JEFF BEACHAM

IN THE
SHADOW
OF
ETERNITY!

**A Candid Look at Holding
on to the Call of God through
Three Cultures, Divorce and Cancer!**

*"When the realization sinks in that Jesus set us free from the
ultimate fear of death, you become fearless. Living or dying
pales into insignificance in the shadow of eternity!"*

In the **Shadow** of **Eternity!**

What Christian Leaders Say About This Book

"History will record my friend Jeff Beacham as one of the stalwart, ground-breaking leaders of the body of Christ in the 20th and 21st Centuries.

Jeff's ability to discern the movements of the hand of God from season to season, combined with his unwavering obedience to his Lord, molded him into a person whom huge numbers of Christians desire to follow.

All this and more becomes highlighted in a captivating manner in 'In the Shadow of Eternity.' As you read this book, you will find yourself drawing nearer and nearer to God."
C. Peter Wagner, Vice-President, Global Spheres, Inc.

"Jeff's book is destined to be a classic for the generations to study and draw strength from, in order to fulfill their God-given callings. It is a roadmap to guide them in running the race for the high calling of Christ Jesus."
Bishop Anne Gimenez, Rock Church International

"I have known Jeff Beacham for more than 17 years, and he has always had a smile on his face, a twinkle in his eye, and an intense passion to see this generation reached with the gospel. And I have watched him persevere with that same attitude through trials and tests of the most severe kind. You will be encouraged by his faith and stretched by his vision!"

Dr. Michael L. Brown, President, FIRE School of Ministry

"Eternity — 'There is an appointed time for everything!' Ecclesiastes 3:1-8

Many years ago I heard a statement from a great leader who, at the time, was faced with the reality of dealing with the end of his life. 'What would you do if you knew you were at the end of this life on earth, and you only had weeks or days to live?' His answer was, 'I would go and plant a tree.'

I pondered this statement in the sea of so many options to choose from. Yet, this great man of God said that he would plant a tree! Later, I found out that this is a common practice in many countries, especially in Israel. Many plant the olive tree, which is known for its oil for lamps so they can provide light. The olive oil also brings purification and the olive tree is known for its hardiness against all kinds of conditions. It also symbolizes fertility. Some olive trees have lived for up to 500 years and longer.

Jeff Beacham's life is like these mighty trees – full of light, separated in holiness to God, hardy and strong against any adversity, and very fruitful. And when Jeff's life is finished here on earth, like the olive tree, there will be signs (fruit) of Jeff's life and ministry here in America and many other nations of the world!

I can say, as a friend for many years, that there is so much oil of anointing that's in this old, tough tree called Jeff Beacham! The Word of God calls us trees, the planting of the Lord!

Jeff, you're a good mate, thanks for all the oil! When you pass, I'll plant an olive tree in Israel in your name! Your friend now and for eternity."
Bishop Bart Pierce, Rock City Church, Baltimore, MD

"Jeff's life and ministry have had a very positive and far-reaching impact in both Australia and America. I will never forget our explosive times together with 'Catch the Fire Down Under.' The reality of his life story will deeply touch your heart as he shares his victories and defeats and, in the end, overcomes."
John Arnott, Founding Pastor and President of Catch the Fire and Overseer of Partners in Harvest Network of Churches

"Jeff Beacham has given us a powerful book about the realities of life and how to live through those realities in victorious faith. Jeff shares the intriguing story of his heritage which, in itself, should inspire young people today to step out and walk in an adventurous trust in God.

I believe Jeff's journey, with all of the ups and downs, will speak to this emerging generation in a way others cannot. His passion of God and commitment to finish the calling and destiny God has for his life is uplifting and inspiring. May the powerful gift of relentless faith fill your heart as you read and then share this book with others. It is something you cannot keep to yourself – it is something to be shared."
Naomi Dowdy, Mentor, Councilor, Pastor, Singapore

"Walking closely with my brother and friend Jeff Beacham is one of the great honors of my life. He walks authentically in an 'overcoming faith' that is real and substantive and never forced or contrived. He is deeply human, and profoundly in touch with Heaven. The gates of hell have not, and will not, prevail against him or his testimony of faith.

This epistle that he writes to the contemporary Church will challenge and strengthen you in tremendous life-giving ways. I am a different and better disciple because I have encountered Jesus, the Living Christ, in the person of His friend, Jeff Beacham."

Robert Stearns, Executive Director, Eagles Wings

"Jeff Beacham has done us all a favor through his telling of his story. Few people could walk through the fires of life and come out on the other side with such faith and joy."

Cindy Jacobs, Generals International

In the Shadow of
Eternity!

A Candid Look at Holding on to the Call of God through Three Cultures, Divorce and Cancer!

Jeff Beacham

In the **Shadow** of **Eternity!**

First Printing

Publishers have allowed this work to remain exactly as the author intended, verbatim, without editorial input.

Ebook 978-1-304-55628-8

Softcover 978-1-304-55592-2

Hardcover 978-1-304-84598-6

Co-Published by:

Firepower Ministries International
2235 Ocean Heights Ave.
Egg Harbor Township, NJ 08234
www.firepowerint.com
firepowerministries@live.com

Revival Waves of Glory Books & Publishing
www.revivalwavesofglory.com
Litchfield, IL

Printed in the United States of America

Acknowledgements

The quality of your family is one of the main deciding factors that determines the quality of your life. As you will learn from this book, I was fortunate to have an adventurous, hard-working and sturdy family background. My parents, Pat and Agnes Beacham, combined stability, talent, artistry, sacrifice and wonderful provision to give their three children a secure upbringing. I am thankful to God for their lives and the foundation they gave me.

New Zealand based evangelist, Barry Smith had a major impact on my early Christian walk. His son, Andrew remains one of my closest friends to this day. I am deeply grateful for the example the Smith family has set for us.

Frank Houston was a true 'father in the faith' to me. The many years of working together in Australia before he passed taught me just about everything I know about the ministry. There's not a day that goes by when you're not in my thoughts, Frank. I'm looking forward to seeing you again in the light of eternity!

I owe a large debt to Joseph Mattera for his embracing a 'new kid on the block' to New York City in 1999. Thank you for your trust ever since.

Walt and Maureen Healy have been there through thick and thin during my American sojourn. I may not have made it through if not for their prayers and steadfastness, standing side by side with us since 1999.

Thank you, Eddie Smith, for your counsel and support in getting this book out. I could not have done it without you.

Johnny and Juanita Berguson, you have been such faithful friends and an unwavering support to me personally and to our ministry ever since we met soon after we moved here from Australia. Thank you also for your help in the cover design and letting folks know about this book through the resources of Kingdom Inc.

Patti Pell has been a key member of my staff since 2000 and the greatest example of faithfulness I know. I am indebted to her for the many hours of proofing it has taken to make this book readable. You are precious!

I am grateful for my former wife of 23 years, Heather, who was an excellent mother raising our five children. I am grateful for my children – Sam, David, Rebekah, Jacob and Isaac – gifts from God to me. I know that the foundation they received, even though it may have been battered by the dealings, twists and turns of life, will eventually shine through. And for that, I'm very thankful!

Finally, what can I say about my wife, Melva? God gave you to me as a precious gift. One of my young colleagues in ministry once remarked, "God must really love you, Jeff, because He gave you Melva!"

Thank you for the sacrifices you have made over the years for the call of God on your life, for the ministry, and for me!

Jeff Beacham

Table of Contents

In the **Shadow** of **Eternity!**

Foreword

Jeff Beacham, a man I have known since 1999, has had the privilege of writing a book that will most likely be remembered as a summary of his final words to his friends, family, and the body of Christ.

He is an amazing man who, in many respects, is also a modern day Job! When he answered the call of Christ upon his life, he both surrendered all and (eventually) lost all – what he has gone through since coming to the USA would have knocked most of us out of the race!

Jeff is a master communicator – both in speech and in writing – and has done a masterful job of giving us a context of his life, culture and the many transitions he has experienced during his walk of faith.

His life story as a rock musician both before and after Christ can be a script for a Hollywood blockbuster! His insights into ministry in Australia, including his time at Hillsong, are fascinating! He also provides important insight regarding the culture shock leaders and their families can go through when they adopt another nation as their primary mission field – especially in the context of better understanding cross-cultural ministry.

Jeff's passionate love for God and people is very evident to all who know him, and in this book he is giving us a gift of insight and wisdom by allowing us to peek into the soul of a man who knows that he is likely living in the final days of his life on earth!

I so appreciate his honesty and transparency, especially in these days when too many leaders are superficial and only deal with surface issues that merely excite the emotions, but fall flat when it comes to preparing people for life's struggles!

This book is also unusual for a minister who moves in both Charismatic and Pentecostal circles, since many in these movements fail to face the fact that not everybody gets healed. That denial of reality has made this book even more valuable for all to read – not just for those grappling with a terminal disease but also for any person dealing with pain, suffering and betrayal of trust, which can be even more painful than a terminal disease!

I thank God for my close friendship with Jeff Beacham! I thank God for this book! I thank God for having the honor of witnessing a leader like him, who never quit under personal pressure or gave up hope even when it seemed as though his whole world was crumbling around him!

Rarely do you ever meet such a man of fire, passion, covenant and commitment on a mission to complete the task the Lord has given him no matter what the cost! He is truly one "tough guy"! As an example of this, even in what seem to be his final days, filled with intense bodily pain, he is working hard to churn out this book for our benefit and for the praise of God!

For those of you who have known Jeff, this book will encourage you to face the stark realities of pain and suffering in this world with courage and hope. For those of

14

you who never met Jeff, this book will enable you to know a man who has remained faithful and fruitful under fire.

I would to God that all of us would have the same tenacity, courage and commitment that Jeff Beacham has exhibited throughout his life.

I encourage you to read this book with the eyes of faith and courage and also to pray for everyone around him, including his family, to fulfill the call and destiny of their life in Christ Jesus.

Joseph Mattera, Founding Pastor of Resurrection Church Brooklyn, NY and Overseeing Bishop of Christ Covenant Coalition

In the **Shadow** of **Eternity!**

Preface

Jeff Beacham is one of the most affable men of God I know. His easy-going style and ability to connect cross-culturally and trans-generationally have made him someone everyone wants to know in the Kingdom. In every sphere he has touched, he is reminiscent of how a lightning rod attracts lightning.

Jeff has a phenomenal ability to attract and gather people to Christ and His Kingdom, and get them to fall in love with Jesus and His purpose in the earth. His rich history has made him the sum total of who he has become in Christ globally today.

He has been graced to touch many of the great streams in God's River of Life that are flowing around the world. The word "apostolic" has many connotations in the current culture of the Church. One that I believe is essential that cannot afford to be overlooked is the reality that to be "apostolic" implies the ability to reproduce.

Reproduction is at the core of everything from evangelism, discipleship, church-planting to leadership development. For the Church to truly be apostolic, it has to remain true to the apostolic Gospel revealed in the Scriptures with all the rich texture it includes, so that it can obtain the same results as revealed in the Book of Acts.

In a day of oversimplification when it comes to theology, Jeff has stood as a pioneer, a thought leader, and a true apostolic father, moving in the generative power of the Holy Spirit to raise up a generation of those who will honor the faith once for all delivered to the saints. His integrity is a cherished strength that all of us who know him benefit from.

All of us have to live life "in the shadow of eternity." Certain things can touch our life unexpectedly and cause us to face extreme challenges that can obscure our vision of what is possible for us in God.

Jeff has had to face a battle for life in the last few years, and yet his vision has not been obscured and his love for Christ, his commitment to the Gospel and to Christ's Kingdom has only intensified. His ability to endure a fiery trial and not have even the "smell of smoke" has been an inspiration to us all.

Each of us intended to leave a legacy behind for others to grown on. All of us have to be mindful of the words of the late C. T. Studd in his well-known poem, "Only One Life."

There are many verses to that well-known poem; however, I want to key in on one particular verse that to me speaks of the example of Jesus in the life of my friend, Jeff Beacham:

> 'Give me Father, a purpose deep,
> In joy or sorrow Thy word to keep;
> Faithful and true what e'er the strife,
> Pleasing Thee in my daily life;
> Only one life, 'twill soon be past,
> Only what's done for Christ will last.'

Jeff has been on an adventure from his beginnings. The spirit of adventure is in his DNA and his family history. That adventurous, fiery spirit refuses to be quenched no matter what he faces.

18

His star continues to burn brightly regardless of the challenges even at this season. He shines as a star with God's endless light in the radiance of Christ, and we are all the better because of it.

A "tome" is a weighty, scholarly book. I would like to suggest that while the book you hold in your hands is a story, it too is a "tome." It reveals the weightiness of God's glory and the scholarship of the Holy Spirit in the life of a unique and treasured man whom God has given as a gift to His Church.

Dr. Mark Chironna, Church on the Living Edge, Mark Chironna Ministries, Orlando, Florida

In the **Shadow** of **Eternity!**

Introduction

Those who have followed my ministry for some time will know that I am no stranger to writing. We have been publishing the monthly FMI Report, documenting the course of our ministry, since 1998. That, along with a library of articles which are all available on our website at www.firepowerint.com, definitely shows no writer's block here.

So, why did it take so long to get this book out?

I confess that I have been delaying obedience to the Lord in this regard! He has been reminding me for some years that this book is a part of my assignment. There is no excuse! However, I take solace that God's will and His timing must be merged for success.

Even recently, at a point when I had completed a little over half the manuscript, I lost steam and put this writing on the shelf for several months, being sorely distracted with declining health, pain and treatments.

That was, until I had a visit from a close friend in ministry who challenged me regarding any God-given assignments that may be in danger of being unfinished, should I pass in the near future. There was only one that immediately sprung to mind – this book!

My friend declared that God would give me the strength and energy to finish the task. I took heed of that word and got the ball up and rolling again!

For those just getting to know us through this book, I trust the semi-autobiographical format will set the scene for how I have made it thus far, through three cultures and some severe trials, leaving you with valuable pointers on how to endure, as a result of what I have learned through my journey with the Lord.

For those who do know us, I trust it will fill in a lot of gaps, answer questions and leave you with hope for the future.

Either way, I believe this book is what He wants for His Body, and what He wants for this time!

Jeff Beacham
Toms River, NJ | 2013

Part One – The Early Years in New Zealand

In the **Shadow** of **Eternity!**

CHAPTER 1
Heritage

Half the World Away

Around the turn of the twentieth century, a young couple from a mountain village in Lebanon, along with their three small children, decided to immigrate to the other side of the world. Their destination – the small 'down under' nation of New Zealand.

This was a bold step for a husband barely out of his teens and his wife who was just eighteen. As was the custom in Lebanon in those days, they married very young.

Their DNA was very much inherited from their Phoenician ancestors, who had once flourished in the area of the Mediterranean that would eventually become Lebanon.

Phoenicia was a sea-faring merchant empire that stretched to the edges of the then-known world, so travel and adventure were in this young couple's blood!

After a long sea voyage through treacherous waters, they settled in the small town of Blenheim, situated at the top of New Zealand's South Island. They chose this location because the only other Lebanese family they knew in New Zealand lived there.

The Peters were relatives from the same mountain village of Beshārrī back home in Lebanon, very close to the Cedars of Lebanon which had trees three thousand years old! The Peters family had made the long and arduous journey to New Zealand some years earlier.

So here they were… half the world away from home in a totally foreign culture; not knowing the language; and separated from family, friends, and everything that was familiar.

Gold Rush

The discovery of gold in this newly settled British colony spurred many mining towns up and down the South Island's west coast, creating an opportunity for the young Lebanese husband and father to spend months on end travelling from town to town by horse and cart, selling pots and pans to the miners.

His young wife stayed behind with her relatives, taking care of the couple's three small children.

Tragedy Strikes

Making his way home from one fateful trip, after being away for about three months, the husband was crossing the bridge over a flooded river not far from home when it unexpectedly collapsed. He, his horse, and cart were suddenly swept away. Sadly, he drowned and all was lost.

His devastated widow was at a loss and could only think of going back home to Lebanon. However, in those days to get there was not just a 24-hour plane ride like it is today. It meant spending many months on a ship, crossing some perilous oceans, at great expense!

Going It Alone

So instead, leaving her three children behind with the relatives, this brave young woman somehow managed to

The Joseph Family, (L to R) Ruby, Margaret, Gabriel, Agnes, Mary and Monsour

find another horse and cart, and off she went by herself for months on end, selling pots and pans to the miners in order to provide for her family.

Only the Lord knows what a young woman alone had to put up with in those rough, lawless gold mining towns. I'm sure she would have many a tale to tell!

However, she seemed to survive intact and after about two years, she had saved enough to take herself and the children back to Lebanon.

Globe Trotters

After several years in her home country, she remarried. Amazingly, she and her new husband, along with the three children from her first marriage, made the long journey back to New Zealand, where they eventually settled in the rural town of Hastings, on the east coast of the North Island.

There she had three more children. The youngest was Agnes, my mother (see photo above)!

Earthquake in the 'Shaky Isles!'

By the late 1920s, my grandfather and grandmother, Mansour and Ruby Joseph, and their family of six children

The 1931 Napier/Hastings Earthquake

had established one of the town's most popular restaurants. The entire family pitched in, even the youngest daughter Agnes, who was approaching her teens.

Then tragedy struck again on Tuesday, February 3, 1931. Life suddenly came to a screeching halt at 10:47am when an earthquake destroyed Hastings and the neighboring coastal town of Napier, killing 256 people! The land shook for a long time and huge portions rose up out of the ocean! To this day, it remains New Zealand's deadliest natural disaster.

At that instant, my mother was riding home from a school function in the car with her mother. Agnes' best friend was also returning home, riding with her mother in the car just ahead of them. Suddenly the road opened up, swallowing the lead car whole, and closed back up again. The car and its occupants were never recovered!

The trauma to the Joseph family, who lost everything when the entire town including their restaurant, was destroyed and to young Agnes, having witnessed the loss of her best friend, is impossible to calculate; however, it took a terrible toll!

The only injury my father sustained that day was when the tile came loose from a roof near where he was standing at school and hit him in the head.

My grandfather, on the other hand, was very fortunate to escape with his life. He had run back into his house to try and retrieve some valuables, when the house began collapsing around him.

Pat Beacham

Today, Napier's airport rests on the land that rose from the sea during the earthquake, with the pre-earthquake shoreline now about a mile inland!

Getting Together During the War Years

Eight years later, New Zealand, as part of the British Commonwealth, entered into World War II and sent her finest young men to fight in Europe and the Middle East.

Among those men was my father, Pat Beacham, who had met Agnes Joseph shortly before at a dance in Hastings. With the urgency of the times, a close bond quickly developed between the two. That bond would remain strong the four years Pat was away, as evidenced by the shoe box

29

filled with love letters they exchanged during that time, and which I later surreptitiously perused in my early teens.

However, the beautiful Agnes had her share of other suitors during the war years, one of them being an American serviceman stationed in New Zealand, who wanted to take her back to the United States after the war. To her credit, Agnes chose the dashingly handsome, if not slightly retiring Pat. She did ultimately go to live in America, but only vicariously through a wayward, but eventually God-loving son!

Getting Together After the War

Pat, a sergeant in the artillery, was wounded twice in campaigns in Egypt and Africa. Having been taught Latin at Catholic school, he quickly adapted that knowledge to learn Italian. Pat spent the remaining years of the war as an interpreter in Italy.

Shortly after Pat's return from war, he and Agnes were married; however, their relationship did not get off to the best start. Pat returned home pretty much emotionally drained from the horrors of war and had virtually nothing to his name.

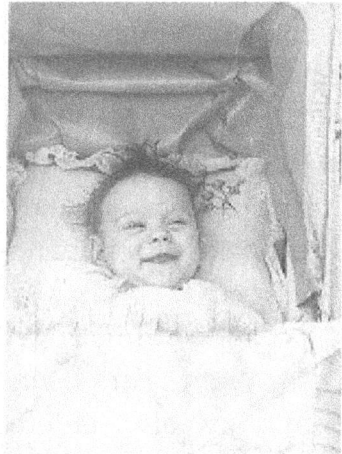

Jeff, 6 months old

The newlyweds moved in with Agnes' parents, which is not exactly the best way to establish the foundation of a marriage. Pat found it very difficult to assert himself and often acquiesced to the strong-willed Agnes, secure in her own element and supported by her family.

By the time they bought their own home a block away, the relationship was established and Agnes pretty much steered the ship. I was the second of four sons, born a few years later. The third son, John unfortunately only lived for 24 hours.

In the **Shadow** of **Eternity!**

CHAPTER 2
Growing up in the 50s and 60s Down Under

The Big Black Buick

My earliest memories are as a four-year-old, going Sunday driving with most of the family in my grandfather's brand new black Buick, one of only two imported from the United States to New Zealand in the early Fifties. That car was so big, just about everyone could fit in it!

My grandfather became very wealthy by buying up a lot of property around Hastings during the war. Because of the imminent threat of Japanese invasion, property was dirt cheap at the time.

However, after the war was over and Japan defeated, the government wanted to honor the returning soldiers by offering them land and houses. Monsour Joseph virtually named his own price and made a fortune!

The story goes that Monsour had heard there was a big black Buick on display at a local car dealership. He was close to seventy at the time, and walked into the dealership in his tatty old clothes.

The salesman, forgivable for thinking the old 'hobo' had no place in this high end dealership, tried to get rid of my grandfather. But Monsour stood his ground and asked in his broken accent how much the car cost. The incredulous salesman, looking down his nose, impatiently quoted "$4,000," a price equivalent to more than the cost of an average home at the time.

The salesman's jaw dropped as my grandfather took out a wad of cash from his back pocket, counted out the $4,000, and drove home that day in his brand new shiny black Buick!

The Old Oak Tree

Another of my earliest memories is as a five-year-old standing by the massive trunk of the old oak tree in the park around the corner from our house and gazing up through the leaves at huge branches that, to me, seemed to almost touch the sky.

That 120-year-old tree became a landmark for me. Every time I have visited my home town in the years since, I

The Old Oak Tree

always go to stand beside its giant trunk under branches that have never seemed to change.

Landmarks are important to our lives, especially in a world of shifting sands, where curve balls and the unexpected can jolt us out of the security of our hopes, dreams, and plans. When things don't turn out as we expected, it's a time to look back to the landmarks of our lives and re-establish our bearings.

That old oak tree never seems to change. It has always been there to help me order my days. In Psalm 90:12, the psalmist asks the Lord to "...teach us to number our days that we may gain a heart of wisdom."

The Legend of the Ghost Bell Ringer!

That little house my parents bought was across the street from St. Joseph's Primary (Elementary) School, right next to the Catholic Church that was a central part of our lives.

The first year at St. Joseph's Catholic School. Jeff middle row far left.

My older brother Greg and I didn't have far to go to school, where we were taught by the nuns. He was two years ahead of me, but we both excelled equally in mischief!

In those days, there was a large sports field at the front of the school, with a small bell house toward the back. The bell was wrung to assemble all the children in the school yard each morning, where the head nun made some announcements and then all the kids marched into their classrooms to the tune of World War II army music. All the nuns lived together in a large house right next to the sports field and bell house.

Always seeking mischief, one night when my brother was about 10 and I was eight, we snuck across the street to the sports field, tied black cotton to the bell ringer, and trailed it right back across to the other side of the sports field, where we hid behind a bush.

When all was quiet, we pulled the cotton and the bell rang! A few seconds later, two nuns appeared at the door of the house where they all lived, puzzled not to see anyone in the bell house. Shaking their heads, they went back inside after a few minutes. No sooner had they gone back inside than we pulled the cotton and

The Sacred Heart Church in the center of town

the bell rang again! The nuns quickly appeared back at the door, certain they would catch the culprit, only to find no one there. Thus began the legend of the ghost bell ringer at St. Joseph's School.

Meeting Jesus

One day, when I was barely 10 years old, the nuns shut down the entire school and took all the kids to a nearby cinema to see a film about the life of Jesus. I was inspired by this amazing story and felt a strange affinity with this 'King of Kings,' sensing a definite call to serve Him, which at the time I thought meant becoming a priest when I was older.

A year or so later, I began my 'apprenticeship' by becoming an altar boy in our local Catholic Church in the center of town, which was also the center of our lives. The church bell was rung faithfully at 12 noon every day. It was heard throughout the entire town and set the order of the day for everyone.

The church was built in 1895, entirely of wood, in the Victorian Gothic architectural style that more suits stone than timber. Sadly, vandals burned it down in the 1990s.

The only thing I didn't like about being an altar boy was getting up at 6am and riding the few miles to the church on my bike on frosty winter mornings.

The Better Side of the Tracks

When I was 10, we moved into a large Tudor style house across town on the better side of the tracks. We had now come to live with the 'well-to-dos.' It was a beautiful two-story house, set in nice grounds on one of the most prestigious streets in town, right across from the racecourse, a very important aspect of all New Zealand communities.

By this time, my father, Pat had graduated from being an insurance agent to being one of two partners in the real estate company, Farrell and Beacham.

The Tudor Style Beacham Family Home

Dad was known as the only realtor who "didn't push!" As a result, his business was very successful up until he retired around the age of 70.

My mother, Agnes, was very talented, beginning her working life in her father's restaurant, then working as the cashier in the cinema next door for many years. She then operated a bridal business from home, making dresses for the entire bridal entourage into the early hours of the morning. She would frequently claim that our life would never have been so good if she had not "slaved to the wee hours of the morning" at the sewing machine for years. However, all efforts to assure her we appreciated everything she had done never seemed to quell her frequent reminders.

Head and Shoulders Above the Rest!

By the time I was 12 and in my last year at St. Joseph's, my Lebanese genes propelled me into an early physical maturity, and I grew a head taller than anyone else at the school.

Playing on the school rugby team met with mixed responses – elation from our team members and parents as I would score almost unhindered, and complaints from the opposition that I was too big!

Elvis Comes to Catholic School

Because of my size, the nuns would sometimes trust me with more responsibility than I could handle. One of those responsibilities was setting up the sound system for the head nun's daily announcements and playing the marching music afterward for the kids to go to their classes.

The Beacham Family, (L to R) Jeff, Agnes, Clive, Pat and Greg.
I was 12 years old in this photo

It was the last day of school that year, and my class would be graduating to begin high school the following year.

This was 1960 and Elvis was still 'King!' I just couldn't resist it! So when the head nun, God bless her heart, had finished speaking, instead of marching music, "One for the money, two for the show, three to get ready, now go cat go!" unexpectedly reverberated through the sound system!

About 300 kids started roaring with laughter, and I was quickly confronted by a red-faced nun saying, "Jeff Beacham, if I give you an inch, you take a mile!" The thing is she couldn't expel me because that was the last day of school!

I still periodically get reminders of that day from those who were there, even after all these years!

In the **Shadow** of **Eternity!**

CHAPTER 3
Moving Through the 'Forrest Gump' Years of Social Change

The Beatles, Hippies, and Drugs

In my first year at high school, my size enabled me to be the sprint champion of the entire school and a member of the 'First Fifteen,' the school's top rugby team. This was usually only attained by seniors.

I was 13 that year… the year I also met my first girlfriend, Margaret, who was 16. She had lost her mother to cancer a few years earlier, but found a surrogate in my mother who, being surrounded by males – my father, brothers and me – needed a 'daughter.' Agnes treated Margaret pretty much like the daughter she never had. We were boyfriend and girlfriend for a couple of years before going our own separate ways, but even to this day, we remain very good friends.

Burned Beatle Boots!

The Beatles came to Catholic School in 1963, and the Sixties social revolution began. My mother burned my Beatle boots that year, but later softened to the 'mop tops' when they cleaned up their act a little bit.

The Beatles had captured the youth culture of the day in the palm of their hands. Unfortunately though, in their search for spiritual fulfillment, they went off to India and sat at the feet of the Maharishi Mahesh Yogi. This opened up a door that became a floodgate for Eastern religions to pour into the West and the New Age movement began… with its hippies, psychedelic drugs, and alternative lifestyles.

The Turning Point

That was a definitive turning point for post-war western culture. All the radical movements it sparked off, such as environmentalism, the peace movement and women's liberation, have now become "main stream."

Now let's backtrack a little. Agnes had arranged for me to have private lessons in speech, drama, music, and fine arts from a young age. I learned how to play the violin, project my voice, was turned on to Shakespeare, and got used to drawing naked people in art class when I was 12!

Phoenician Genes

Those 'Phoenician' genes I'd inherited would not be kept silent for long. When I was 17, I left home in rebellion and moved to New Zealand's capital city of Wellington in pursuit of adventure.

The plan was to go to art school, but that didn't work out. Instead, I took a series of menial jobs to support myself and got fully immersed in the hippie culture for several years.

Somehow or other, I survived that time, although many of my contemporaries did not! I didn't come out unscathed, however. There were several attempts on my life, and I was confronted with the overt violence and depravity of the drug culture and inner city life... a difficult transition for a 'farm' boy from a rural area.

Music

When I was 11, I had learned to play the drums a little. Following those lost teen years, I picked up music again. After playing in a number of bands and touring New Zealand professionally for several years, in 1974 I boarded a plane to Australia in search of more adventure, but for the most part to advance my musical career. All I took with me was one small suitcase and a drum kit.

It was not as big a step as my grandmother had taken more than 70 years earlier, but it sure was a huge culture shock for me!

In the **Shadow** of **Eternity!**

Part Two – The Middle Years in Australia

In the **Shadow** of **Eternity!**

CHAPTER 4
Leaving Behind the Land of Hobbits and Chasing Sex, Drugs, and Rock 'n Roll in the Land of Oz

The Great Southern Land

A ustralia was the 'big smoke' for a 'kiwi' boy from a country only a little larger in area than the United Kingdom and with just over three million people at the time.

Small as it may have been, New Zealand had produced some 'world firsts' with scientist Earnest Rutherford being the first to split the atom, Sir Edmond Hillary the first to climb Mt. Everest, and other notables like Peter Snell, a double gold Olympian medal winner.

Australia, however, had a relatively larger music industry, even though its population was only 18 million people on an island continent slightly larger in area than the United States.

Arriving in Sydney about as green as a new spring leaf, things did not go as I had hoped that first year. Even though I had some good music industry connections made available by a well-established musician from my home town, who had moved to Australia some years before, I was too naïve to take proper advantage of them.

After playing in several bands around the city, I eventually co-founded a new band, Southern Cross. We toured, did TV appearances, and recorded an album that is still very popular amongst the European alternative classic rock scene.

Travolta and Bee Gees

Southern Cross

After several years touring and doing 'session work' in studios for other bands, the hedonistic disco scene of the mid-Seventies pretty much sucked the air out of rock music for a time. This, in turn, quelled my passion for music and I took a 'furlough.'

I had always been interested in movies from a young age, so I applied for a job as a projectionist and editor at the Australian Censorship Board in downtown Sydney. I worked there for several years, along with assisting a Jewish film distributor part time, and working in a cinema nights and weekends, just like my mother used to do.

Being an Aussie

I hadn't lost my love for physical fitness, so every day I would take a bus from the beach suburb of Coogee into the city for work, and then run the 10 miles home at the end of the day.

By this time, I had been living in Australia for nearly eight years, and I was definitely becoming an 'Aussie!'

It was then that I embarked on a spiritual journey. Desperate for meaning and answers after finding myself in a spiritual desert left over from years of hedonism through sex, drugs, and rock 'n roll, I began studying all the world's great faiths and many esoteric beliefs.

"The Late Great Planet Earth"

Like many of my generation raised on Cold War fears of global nuclear annihilation and overpopulation, Hal Lindsey's book *The Late Great Planet Earth* found fertile ground in my heart and a seed was sown that would later germinate through another man's ministry.

In the **Shadow** of **Eternity!**

CHAPTER 5
Conversion and Vision

B arry Smith had more than his share of uniqueness as a human being. Typifying the New Zealand version of the rugged individualist, Barry had grown up as part of the Brethren Church and did missionary work in the islands of the Pacific. On a preaching trip to Samoa as a young man, he met a very pretty young Samoan woman named May and later married her.

Barry and May developed a ministry centered on the End Times and traveled all around Australasia doing evangelistic crusades. They took their four young children with them most of the time. It was one of their visits to a church in the inner city Sydney suburb of Darlinghurst that changed my life forever!

Preaching Without Words

Four months earlier, I had become friends with a young couple. The husband had taken a job working with my wife at the time. She noticed that when the other employees headed off to the pubs of downtown Sydney at lunchtime, this young man would just quietly sit at the back of the shop and read a Bible for the lunch hour. After about three days, curiosity got the better of her. She couldn't resist the urge to ask him why he was doing that when everyone else was getting tipsy over lunch.

That opened the door for this young Christian man to share his faith with my wife. She, in turn, would come home and share that with me. As an unsaved person, my first response was, "Who does this guy think he is, trying to convert my wife?"

However, over the next few months, we became very close with this Christian couple. They gave us a video set of Barry Smith's ministry. I watched all five of the videos non-stop over an entire weekend and was absolutely amazed!

From my own studies, I was already familiar with a lot of the things he spoke about, but he had the missing piece... the one piece that tied everything together... the piece I had been missing all those years of searching – JESUS!

After watching all those videos that weekend, I resolved in my heart to begin following this man, Jesus. Still, it would take several months before I walked up the aisle of Christian Life Centre church in Darlinghurst at Barry's first meeting to publicly give my life to Christ. That was in 1983!

The Big Clean Up

In the months leading up to that life-changing night, God had done a huge work in me, cleaning up my heart from alcohol, drugs, swearing, and the like. And I began to treat my wife more like a Christian man should!

The amazing thing was that I now couldn't blaspheme the name of Jesus any longer as I had done every few words for most of my life. His name had now become special and precious to me, and I found myself jealously defending it.

My cleaning up was not an easy process. I remember many nights, for weeks on end, filled with nightmares and terrifying dreams of contending with a being of unimaginable horror, who I can only think was the devil himself. The only way I could overcome his tight grip on my soul was to declare the name of Jesus at the top of my voice in my dreams. Every time I did that, he would wince, be diminished, and withdraw!

Getting Planted

When I publically gave my life to Christ, a lot of the tough work in me had already been done, and I was looking to grow fast spiritually.

The following Tuesday night, we found the 'home fellowship' group nearest to our area and attended our first meeting. We were strongly encouraged to do so by the altar call worker who counseled us the night we were 'saved.'

We immediately bonded with the fine young people at the home fellowship group. That was a major component of our early Christian growth. Friendships grew, many of which have endured to this day.

I was in my early thirties when I got baptized shortly after making my public commitment to Christ. I came up out of the water speaking in tongues.

Phil Hills was the guest speaking at the church that night. He pastored Richmond AOG in Melbourne and was a close friend of Frank Houston, pastor of Christian Life Centre. Phil began to prophesy over me, saying that I would preach God's Word to nations.

Prophetically Commissioned

Part of me was a little overwhelmed with that 'word' because I was a newborn babe in Christ. How could this be? Another part of me was not surprised at all. Looking back over my life... with my training in speech, drama, art, and music... I knew that God had been preparing me to serve Him from a young age.

Christian Life Centre

Frank Houston had been Superintendent of the AOG in New Zealand for 19 year before moving to Sydney, Australia in 1977 to pioneer Christian Life Centre (CLC). There were nine adults and five children at their first service in Sydney's eastern suburbs!

Shortly afterward, several others followed him from New Zealand, including his natural son, Brian, and a spiritual son, Paul De Jong. Brian became the Associate Pastor at CLC and Paul started off as the Youth Pastor.

Creative Ministries

Trevor King had been a professional musician before getting 'saved' shortly after the church began; he became CLC's first full-time worship leader. Amongst other things, Trevor had played in the Andy Gibb Band. Andy was the brother of the three Bee Gees and would tragically end his life some

Trevor King

54

years later.

Contemporary Christian music was in an underdeveloped state at that time, but Trevor was determined to make a difference. He prayed that God would send him some other professional musicians to join his quest.

Air Supply, David Moyse, second from right

Shortly thereafter, those prayers were answered when David Moyse, lead guitarist with the world-famous group 'Air Supply,' walked forward to give his life to Christ at one of CLC's Sydney Town Hall outreaches, which were held every Sunday night for a month in the summer of 1982.

Around that time, George McArdle, bass player with 'The Little River Band,' another world-famous group, got saved, along with some professional lighting and sound guys.

So here we all were; gathered in answer to Trevor's prayer.

Within a few short weeks of being saved, I had joined the 'Creative

The Little River Band, George McArdle, rear center

Ministries' team and began to play drums again; this time not for sex, drugs and rock 'n roll, but in the service of the Lord!

This group of professionals all shared Trevor's vision to write and produce worship music that would set trends for the world to follow, rather than what we saw at that time with the church coming along 30 years after the world had already been doing it, gingerly dipping its toes into the water saying, "Is it safe to go in now?"

We actually, some would say naively, believed what the Word said when it declared we were the "head and not the tail!"

Hillsong

Early in 1984, Frank's son Brian was sent to plant Hills Christian Life Centre in Sydney's western 'Hills' district. Geoff Bullock, one of Trevor's protégés, went with Brian to be the worship leader.

In 1985, Geoff wanted to run a weekend workshop for musicians, singers, lighting and sound people. He enlisted the help of the 'city musos' to join together with his team. Since it was all about music and in the Hills district, he called it 'Hillsong.' About 200 showed up to be instructed and encouraged by some of the best around.

Brian Houston, circa 1985

It was such a success, the following year 400 turned out, and the year after that there were nearly 1,000! At that point, it became an annual conference for the entire church, including sessions on leadership, evangelism, and spirit life.

The Hillsong conferences began to showcase the prolific song writing of Geoff Bullock, with classics such as "The Power of Your Love" and "The Great South Land of the Holy Spirit," the original name for Australia given by the Portuguese.

Live worship albums from the conferences quickly spread all over Australia and began to be popular in Europe and eventually worldwide!

Then in 1995, when Geoff Bullock left Hills Christian Life Centre, everyone thought the great worship would come to an end, but a young back-up singer on the worship team stepped up. Darlene Zschech became the new worship leader, and the rest is history!

Soon after, Darlene wrote "Shout to the Lord." It became a worldwide phenomenon and really put Hillsong on the global map.

Darlene Zscheck

All over the world, Hillsong became a household name, but no one had heard of Hills Christian Life Centre, so in the early 2000s, the name of the church was changed to what everyone knew it as – Hillsong Church!

Sometimes the vision God gives us is too much for one generation. The baton has to be passed to those coming up. Today, Hillsong regularly has the biggest selling albums in Australia... period... both secular and Christian! It truly is setting trends that the world will follow!

In the **Shadow** of **Eternity!**

CHAPTER 6
Boot Camp

I was saved in October 1983. At the start of 1984, CLC founded a very unique local church-based Bible college, the International Institute for Creative Ministries (IICM). I was so excited about this because it was a full-time school where you could study theology and the arts. You could major in music and minor in theology, or vice versa. Or you could do fine arts, photography, song, dance, or drama.

I wanted desperately to go to IICM, but several naysayers said I was 'too young in the Lord' to go. I knew I was just a 'baby,' but I still felt a strong drawing to sign up for the two-year, full-time course.

We were a young family with a small child and even though I could not deny the calling, I had not yet grown the faith that would be needed to give up my job and trust God!

A Rhema Word

I remember one night, when I was waiting on God to show me if He wanted me to go to IICM or not, I received my first 'rhema' word. I opened my Bible and my eyes fell upon a scripture in Luke 8:50, which said, "Fear not, just believe...." Those words jumped right out of the page and stood up in front of me like a neon sign. I was amazed. From that point on, going to IICM was not a choice, but a command!

Leaving behind all the naysayers, I left my job, signed up full-time for two years, and began a walk of trusting in God that I'm still following today, even if those were baby steps back then.

My Best Friend

There were 35 full-time students from all walks of life and age groups in that inaugural year of IICM; however, most were young people.

On the first day, I was really pleased to see the son of Barry Smith as one of my fellow students. I had loved hearing Andy Smith and his future wife, Saskia, sing together at the meetings his father had at CLC, where I went forward to publically commit to Christ.

Andy was 18 and I was 34, but we hit it off right from the start and became almost inseparable.

It wasn't long before he moved in with us in our rented house at Coogee, the beach suburb of Sydney.

He had been commuting two hours every morning to get to each day's opening chapel before classes and then another two hours to get back to where he was staying in Sydney's West. He was exhausted! We lived only 15 minutes away from the college, so it was a welcome relief for Andy.

Working for the Church

I also became close with Trevor King and after just a few months into my first year at IICM, he offered me the part-time position of administrator for the Creative Ministries Department, which at that time was comprised of about 120 people, including musicians, singers, dancers, puppeteers, drama performers, and the choir.

This meant I would spend mornings at the college, most afternoons doing administrative work for Creative Ministries, then rush home to spend time with my young family, and stay up until 1 or 2am studying.

I also started a home fellowship group that met at our house. It quickly grew to about 60 people in my first year as a Christian. We eventually split it into three separate groups a while later.

The two years of study at IICM were intense and included my pitiful attempt at singing – a requirement of my music minor. Andy and some other students were unable to stifle their giggles and had to leave the room when that recital took place. As a singer, I made a good drummer!

However, I was there mainly to learn the Word, because I knew right from the start that I was called to preach.

The Faith Walk

During the two years at Bible School, we had three students staying with us, some of whom we supported, yet the rent was always paid, the fridge was always full of food, and our gas tank was

Frank Houston (L) congratulates Jeff for graduating from IICM

never empty. It was a great growth spurt in faith for me!

No sooner had I graduated, than I received a call from the senior pastor, Frank Houston one morning, offering me a position as his personal assistant. So for the next four years, I traveled with Frank, did all his administrative work, and set up "Walk in Wisdom." The latter was a travelling road show with its own staging, lighting, sound system, and our top musicians.

I would set up city-wide 'crusades' involving as many churches as possible. Frank would preach at the night meetings and during the day sessions, he'd instruct leaders with lessons learned from planting one of Australia's fastest growing churches at that time.

Over the course of the next two and a half years, the "Walk in Wisdom" team traveled three or four times a year to different parts of Australia.

Those four years with Frank taught me more than Bible College ever did!

Pastoring and the Australian AG

Frank Houston was the Superintendent of the Assemblies of God in New South Wales, one of Australia's six states, and he was also a member of the National AOG Executive.

This afforded me the opportunity to get close personally to many senior leaders; something that helped me mature spiritually very quickly.

After about two years of serving Frank, I also became an 'area pastor' at CLC for the western portion of Sydney. There were people coming to our church from all over the city, and we had divided up our home fellowship system into North, South, East and West.

The East was limited by the Pacific Ocean, but the West was a seemingly endless suburban sprawl! I had about 400 people to pastor, and it would take all day to get around to see just a handful.

All of this was on top of my already busy schedule of being Frank's assistant and still being part of the creative ministries, playing drums during services.

The Birthing of Firepower Ministries International

In July of 1989, I had a dream one night where I saw myself in the middle of a huge field covered with bundles of straw every few yards. I had a flaming torch in my hand, and I was running around lighting each bundle. I awoke after that dream with the word 'firepower' on my mind. That is where I got the inspiration to found a ministry named Firepower Ministries International.

The field was the world ready for harvest; the bundles of straw represented churches in all nations; I was the revivalist who was to set them on fire!

By this time, I had been keenly observing how Frank would minister and preach with an emphasis on the gifts of the Holy Spirit, which he in turn had gleaned from his mentor, Ray Bloomfield.

Ray had led some revivals in New Zealand before moving to Canada in the Sixties. Frank's early background had been in the Salvation Army, but his meeting up with Ray was like hitting a Pentecostal tractor trailer at 60 miles an hour! Frank received the baptism of the Holy Spirit through Ray, and it set his diminutive frame on fire!

In the early years of my Christian experience, I also became very close with Barry Smith and his family. We attended several of his training camps on their rural property in New Zealand's South Island, ironically in exactly the same area where my grandmother had originally settled. These camps were short-term training intensives on Bible prophecy.

I was beginning to hone my skills as a Spirit-filled, on fire, Bible prophecy preacher!

I was also very passionate about reaching the next generation and got involved with Youth Alive, the AOG's youth ministry, which would attract tens of thousands of young people to rallies all over Australia.

World Expo 1988

In 1988, Trevor King was asked to produce the only Christian concert for the World Expo that was held in Brisbane that year. He called in his 'mates' David Moyse, George McArdle and me to form a band. But we had no front man... until we found a young singer/songwriter named Steve Grace.

We combined some of our songs with his and rehearsed for three days. On the night of the concert on the River Stage in the middle of the Expo, which was on the Brisbane River's west bank right in the middle of the city, 30,000 people showed up for the largest Christian concert in Australia's history, up to that time.

The Steve Grace Band, World Expo, Brisbane '88

Soon after, the Steve Grace Band, as it became known, went on to record "Children of the Western World," the largest selling Christian album of that year.

Touring with Newsboys

We also did a concert tour of several major cities in Australia with the Newsboys, Randy Stonehill, and Phil Keaggy.

Later that year, I set up a tour of Youth Alive with our band backing Jeff Fenholt who, before meeting Christ, was a former singer with Black Sabbath and also played Jesus in "Jesus Christ Superstar" on Broadway.

We had Prince's former bodyguard, Big Chick, with us on that tour. His testimony of finding Christ led many to Christ.

Big Chick

This was all a tremendous experience, which I had to juggle with all my other responsibilities assisting Frank and pastoring at the church. Shall we say, I had my hands really full all of the time!

Sons in the Faith

As if I was not already busy enough, from 1989 onward, I began travelling to different parts of Australia to start fulfilling the vision of FMI by preaching at different churches roughly two weekends each month.

Over the next few years, I developed my combined emphasis of prophecy and the Holy Spirit, and we saw thousands of people give their lives to Christ.

We then extended FMI's reach to other neighboring nations such as New Zealand, Indonesia, Korea, Malaysia, the Philippines and Fiji. Eventually, I was traveling to a different nation and all around Australia every month.

FMI began as a department of Sydney Christian Life Centre in 1989 and did not become its own entity until late

1995. At that time, we began producing our own TV program, "Let the Fire Burn." It aired on GOD TV and was seen in over 25 nations in Europe.

Our Bible College had a name change when, at Frank Houston's invitation, Robert Fergusson moved his family from Nottingham in the United Kingdom to Sydney to head up the college. Robert changed the name to Aquila.

Many of our finest young people did the two year course and, upon graduation, some were channeled into internship at the church.

One day, a young graduate by the name of Todd Rigby showed up at my office and sheepishly declared that God had told him he was to serve me as an intern. He naively thought that pastors had a 'cushy' job; they only had to work one hour a week preaching and, the rest of the time, they sat around in the office with their feet up, drinking coffee all week long!

I told Todd I would think about it, but also warned him that I ran pretty fast and if he wanted to run with me, he'd have to keep up! "No problem at all!" he declared. But once I told him I'd take him on, he was only with me for about four days before he was ready to throw in the towel! Todd learned quickly that ministry was hard work... and lots of it!

Todd had taken over from another son in the faith, Michael Fuller, who worked with FMI for a few years prior to Todd coming alongside. Together, we traveled and ministered over most of Australasia and a strong bond grew between us.

Today, they are both still like sons to me. Whenever I return to Australia, we always catch up and have a big laugh about some of the experiences we shared together on the road.

On one of our last visits, we had dinner with Todd and his wife, Michelle. Todd is a lot older now and married with two kids, but he still retains some of that refreshing naivety, which is so endearing. Over dinner he remarked,

Todd Rigby with one of his daughters

"You know Jeff, when God speaks to me; He speaks in your voice!" We couldn't stop laughing when he said that, but inside, I thought to myself, "What a responsibility!"

The old look to the young for energy; the young look to the old to hear God's voice!

In the **Shadow** of **Eternity!**

CHAPTER 7
The Fire Ignites

The Fire Ignites in Toronto!

E arly in September 1994, we began to catch wind of a revival that had been going on since January that year at a small church near the end of the runway at the airport in Toronto in the province of Ontario, Canada.

People had started to travel there from all over the world, lining up for hours to get into the nightly meetings at the Toronto Airport Vineyard Church, which could only accommodate about 200 people. Hungry souls went there seeking to be renewed, refreshed, and revived. Time Magazine published an article about the revival, which fueled it even more.

I was in the middle of meetings at a Melbourne church at the time, and I felt a clear leading from God to go to the Toronto Revival the very next week.

This was going to be an enormous step of faith for me, but I got Frank's blessing and on short notice found the airfares, shuffled my schedule around, and found babysitters to take care of our young family of five children for the 10 days we would be away. Everything fell into place and off we went; those Phoenician genes kicking in again, looking for adventure!

We had set aside a week or so to catch what was going on there. Truthfully, I was very dry spiritually at the time after continuously pouring out everything in me while on the road for several years.

We were the first Charismatic ministers from Australia to arrive in Toronto, and we arrived right in the middle of a healing conference they were holding at a local hotel. It was bedlam!

I made it my business to stay close to Vineyard's senior pastor, John Arnott, as he went around the big ballroom 'soaking' people in God's presence. Others on their leadership team were doing the same, including John's wife, Carol. The floor was just a sea of bodies as folks from all over the world went 'out under the power' of the Holy Spirit.

Back at the little church, meetings were held morning and night after that… and we were at every one! One night, John asked me to come up to the front and testify about what God was doing in me, and then he prayed over me. I dropped like a rock and had a powerful time with God, on the floor doing 'carpet time!'

On our final day there, I had a private meeting with John and asked him to come to Australia the following May for a Catch the Fire Conference in Sydney. He agreed, then we went back out to the meeting to get prayed for one last time before leaving for the airport to catch our plane back to Australia.

When we left the church in our rental car a short time later, we were so 'drunk in the Spirit,' it was as if I had drunk a whole bottle of whiskey! Pulling out of the church parking lot, I merrily drove about a quarter of a mile down the wrong side of the road, while tires squealed as the oncoming cars careened to a halt. Praise God; He was in control. No one was injured, and folks back at the church were laughing as they watched this mayhem through the window.

The Fire Ignites in Australia!

We arrived back in Australia in time to attend the CLC Annual Church Retreat in Sydney's northern beaches area a few days later.

Although, we weren't scheduled to minister, everyone knew where we had been. There was an air of expectation and anticipation that at some point we would 'release the blessing.' After Frank had finished speaking at the Saturday night meeting, people started to drift off to other parts of the retreat center to socialize. A few hungry folk stayed around, and we began to 'soak' them. It was like lighting a match to dry tinder! The worship team began to have a hard time keeping it together as spontaneous laughter broke out while they were playing, and people started falling all over the place. This went on for about 45 minutes! The commotion started drawing people back from other parts of the retreat center to see what was going on.

It was a shemozzle! People were all over the floor laughing their heads off or deep in communion with the Lord. Some of the main leaders were a little skeptical to begin with. We were not strangers to seeing the Holy Spirit move under Frank's ministry, but this was another level! That night changed everything!

A short time later, Frank decided we should have a special retreat for the leaders of CLC to learn more about this new move of the Spirit. It started with a teaching I gave on what I had experienced and learned in Toronto. By that time, at my urging, two of our other elders, Robert Fergusson and Jonathan Wilson, had also gone to Canada and were highly impacted.

The three of us shared about our experiences and then began to pray and 'soak' all the leaders one by one. People would be on the floor for a long time. There was a tangible presence of the Lord present, and a strong weightiness came upon everybody. At one point, Frank got stuck to the wall, almost as if someone had put a huge suction cup on his back. Later that night, he was so 'drunk in the Spirit' that we had to carry him off to his room, where he laughed all night long and kept everyone awake!

The Ring of Fire Down Under

A short time before all these events, Steve Penny, a highly credible prophet and member of the AOG National Executive Team, had given a prophecy that there would be a ring of fire surrounding Sydney. This proved to be true in the natural and the spiritual!

The bush fires around Sydney were particularly destructive that year and actually formed a circle around the city. However, my ministry schedule from October 1994 until early 1995 also formed a circle of churches around the outer reaches of the city.

As I visited each church, an unprecedented level of Holy Ghost fire was released. In one of those churches, I received an offering one night to send the pastors of several churches to Toronto. They came back revolutionized!

Catch the Fire Down Under

In May of 1995, I hosted the "Catch the Fire Down Under" Conference at CLC Sydney. We were expecting so many to come that we built a special, temporary auditorium in our parking lot, as well as two other overflows in other parts of the building. A live video feed was piped into each overflow area. Over 3,000 attended from all over Australia, New Zealand, and the Pacific Islands. This was twice the capacity of our building!

I color-coded registrants and rotated them from session to session between all rooms, which gave everybody equal time in the main auditorium. Every day, people lined up for nearly two hours beforehand to get in. We had not previously seen the depth of hunger in the hearts of the people that we were experiencing at this conference. Attendees came from all denominations, including mainline, Evangelical, Charismatic, and Pentecostal.

John and Carol Arnott were our keynote speakers. In each meeting, they imparted the 'Toronto Blessing,' as it was referred to. There were also special meetings where John and Carol taught pastors on how to pastor revival. Their teaching was gleaned from their personal experience, having held nightly meetings at their church nonstop over the past 18 months, at that point in time.

Like all moves of God, controversy was not far behind. Some prominent leaders in the Body of Christ around the world were supportive of what was happening in Toronto; others were not. It was a tough time for the Arnotts when they were disassociated from the Vineyard

Movement some time later, but over the next few years, they set up a global movement of churches.

Rodney Howard-Browne

South African Evangelist, Rodney Howard-Browne, moved to America in the mid-Eighties and had a huge impact on the Pentecostal/Charismatic community. Hosted by Christian City Church (CCC), he visited Australia in early 1995. Senior Pastor, Phil Pringle, knowing that my ministry had taken on a whole new dimension after I came back from Toronto, invited me to minister at his church the week before Rodney was due to arrive. The power of God hit the place like a bomb that night. When Rodney began his meetings at CCC, there were about 2,000 leaders present.

Rodney was invited to be the keynote speaker at the Biannual National AOG Conference in Brisbane that year. It was a blow out! Andrew Evans was the National Superintendent; I remember him, and the rest of the Executive Team, all testifying about how they had been impacted by God through Rodney's ministry. What really stood out was team member, Brian Houston's testimony. Brian declared he had "watched himself go from being the most radical member of the Executive Team to the most conservative overnight!"

CHAPTER 8
The Long Road to Obedience

I felt the first stirrings in my heart that one day we would relocate our ministry to the United States in 1989, the year Firepower Ministries International was founded.

The only person I mentioned it to was an American missionary to Australia, who I had helped in getting permanent residency for himself and his family. I asked him privately what he would think about someone feeling the Lord was calling them to go to America. His answer surprised me! "I would have to say they had questionable motives," he said. I asked why, to which he replied, "In America, there is a church on every street corner. We don't need missionaries there!" His words definitely put a damper on my enthusiasm, but I kept the seed in my heart, where it lay more or less dormant until 1995.

First Call

Most weeks, Frank Houston and I would meet for an hour to catch up. This had been going on for years and combined with our regular lunches, I learned just about everything I know about the ministry during those times. He never had a list of bullet points or an agenda when we met; with Frank, it was more caught than taught!

Every week, he would talk about this and that, then always end our time by saying something like, "Well, unless you've got something else to talk about, I guess I'll see you next week."

On one occasion toward the end of 1995, I said, "Well yes! I do have something to talk about… I think the Lord might be calling us to go to America!" Thinking I was joking, Frank started laughing, while I on the other hand, had a very sober look on my face. He said, "You're serious!" To which I replied, "Yes I am." "No, no; I couldn't possibly let you do that. I need you here too much!" he retorted. "I wouldn't go without your blessing, so take a week to think and pray about it and see what the Lord says, and let's talk about it when we meet next week," I countered.

We had our usual meeting the following week and Frank talked about everything but that! Then came his usual, "Well, unless you've got something else to talk about, I guess I'll see you next week." I replied, "You know what we have to talk about!" "I couldn't get anything," he said. I responded "Okay; I wouldn't dare go without your blessing, so I'll put it on the shelf!"

And I did! For the next four years, I got on with my life, and the ministry continued to grow. I was traveling all over Australia and to a different nation every month; our TV show was being broadcast over 25 nations.

Finally, in May of 1998, God really got on my case! But I'll come back to that later.

That January, I had been invited to minister at the annual Senior Leader's Retreat for the Elim Movement – the largest Pentecostal/Charismatic movement in the United Kingdom. Due to ticketing, I had to fly east of Australia across the United States of America to get there, rather than the shortest distance, which was west... so I decided to break up my trip by stopping in New York City.

I had met Dr. Michael Brown through the Pensacola Revival and had invited him to minister in Australia for several conferences. We became good friends. At that point in time, I had ministered in the United States several times; I was up and down the West Coast and in the South, but I had never been to the Northeast. I contacted Michael to see if he knew anyone in the New York area who might have an interest in me ministering during my weekend stopover. He said he was close with a church in New Jersey that might want me to come.

Touch Down in the Northeast

After a 24-hour flight from Australia, I arrived at JFK Airport in New York City in the middle of a storm on Friday, January 23, 1998.

That weekend, we had an amazing Sunday at The Church of Grace and Peace in New Jersey. The church is led by Walt Healy, a close associate of Dr. Michael Brown. The morning service went for four hours! The entire church responded with a deep hunger for revival. Walt's desire to see the Northeast of America ablaze with the Fire of the Holy Ghost meant that he had canceled his normal program and was only having people in his pulpit who shared his passion for revival.

The end of the service resembled a battlefield as people were impacted by the Holy Spirit, with the young adults demonstrating the greatest hunger. I had ministered to them the night before when, on a couple hours notice, Pastor Healy decided to have an unplanned meeting. When we arrived that night, the street was packed with cars... the young people had come from all over the area!

The Sunday night meeting was very well attended, even though it was "Super Bowl Sunday," which is usually the quietest night of the year for American churches, since it is the biggest football finale in the nation, with more people watching it than the Olympics.

God's Spirit moved even more powerfully that night than at the morning service. Several of the young people shared testimonies of how their lives had been completely turned around overnight, just through one touch from the Lord. They told of deliverance from drugs and alcohol and a dramatically increased desire to see the lost saved.

The whole church responded to the call of "If My people who are called by My name...." (2 Chronicles 7:14) and they repented on behalf of their nation as I exhorted them with the only hope for America being a Great Awakening of the same type that Jonathan Edwards saw in his time.

Over the course of the day, about 100 responded to the altar call for the first time or to get right with God.

The Transition Emerges

I was scheduled to make two more trips to the United States that year – to minister in Toronto in April and Pensacola in September. Pastor Healy asked me to 'piggy back' two more times of ministry with his church in Toms River, New Jersey along with those visits. During that time, a strong bond developed between us and The Church of Grace and Peace leadership team.

I had quite a few ministry friends in America, but I knew that if relocating our ministry and family stateside was going to have any chance of success, there would have to be a church that would 'receive us.' It became apparent that this church might be the one!

Backed Into a Corner

Now back to God getting on my case! In May of 1998, during an intense time of worship at a conference in Melbourne, Australia, I heard Him clearly say to me, "Well....?" I hate it when God backs you into a corner and hits you with that word, because you know something big is about to hit! "I've called you to go to America but, for the last nine years, you've been thinking of every excuse you could to get out of it! If you want to stay in Australia, you'll do okay; but if you go to America, I won't promise it will be easy, but I will bless you. Are you going to obey Me or what? Just give Me a yes or no right now!"

In fear and trepidation, I managed to squeak out a "Yes; alright, I'll do it!" That was possibly the most momentous decision I've ever made in my life.

About a week later, I scheduled a special meeting to tell Frank about all this. I was about to knock on the door of his office, when suddenly the door flew open and Frank stood there and announced, "You're going to America, aren't you?" We went in and sat down and then I said it again, "But I still won't go without your blessing."

Frank confessed that he knew it was God the first time I had talked to him about going to America four years earlier, but that he had let his "own natural feelings get in the way."

Timing and Destiny

It's one thing to know God's will; it's another thing to get the timing right! Moses found out his destiny when he was 40 years old, but he missed the timing and ran ahead of God, blew it and had to wait another 40 years for the wheel to turn and bring him to the point where destiny and timing intersected to fulfill God's purpose for his life.

If I had ignored Frank's constraints four years earlier and just went ahead and relocated to America, "obeying God rather than man," as one independent leader said, rebuking me soon after I eventually arrived here, it would have been a disaster!

For a start, there was no church at that time that was prepared to sponsor and embrace us, and even though I knew it was God's will all along, I also needed to have the blessing of my elders and peers.

We talked through the details with Frank for several weeks and it was decided that we would be sent as missionaries to America. At the same time, I was talking extensively with Pastor Healy and others about the process of being received by them. Eventually, official letters were exchanged between Frank and Walt and the die was set.

However, there was one crucial piece of the puzzle that needed to be put in place – that was getting visas for our entire family.

It took me from June 1998 until early 1999 to prepare the applications for seven R1 (religious workers) visas. During that time, very few people were privy to our intended relocation. Everything depended on getting those visas and nothing could be made public until then.

Early in February, that puzzle piece came into place and six months of wading through bureaucratic red tape culminated in all our passports being stamped with visas in less than 30 minutes one day.

It was then that Frank said we needed to let the CLC staff know first. We had a special staff meeting that afternoon, and it was very bittersweet. It was hard for all of us to stay composed after working together for 16 years.

Brian Houston made it to that meeting on short notice, driving an hour and a half to get there from Hills CLC church, as it was known then. His presence was greatly appreciated.

Dismantling a Lifetime

It took me a year to dismantle everything I had built up over a lifetime down under. But a true disciple of Christ knows that if you want to go to the next level He has for you, you must be prepared to die to everything on the present level!

When promotion comes from the Lord, it can often seem like you're moving into something less. However, if you have been faithful to raise up disciples to replace yourself, God will never take you to less; He'll bring you to something greater in His economy.

David and Gaye Crafts had come to Australia from the small town of Te Puke in New Zealand in 1984. Soon thereafter, they showed up at my home fellowship group and told me that prior to arriving in Australia, they had received a prophetic word along the lines that they would be discipled for a time by a leader who would raise them up to the next level.

Dave was a carpenter and soon after arriving in Australia, he established his own construction company. His wife was my administrator for many years, until we left for America. Gaye was absolutely outstanding at her job. Dave and Gaye also became very close personal friends of ours.

Dave was employed as a pastor at CLC Sydney after we left for America. Not long after that, we spoke on the phone. He expressed a great frustration with pastoring. As a builder, he was used to doing a day's work, then stepping back at 'knock off time' and getting an instant sense of fulfillment.

I explained to him that was not the case with taking care of people! Sometimes you never saw much progress and a lot of the time, none at all! The test of pastoring is to keep on going, even if you don't see much fruit. It took Dave a while, but he did get used to it and is a vital part of the Hillsong pastoral staff today.

Part Three – The Sprint to the Finishing Line in the USA

In the **Shadow** of **Eternity!**

CHAPTER 9
Overcoming Second Culture Shock

W̲e arrived at Newark Airport in New Jersey on April 6, 1999 after the 24-hour flight from Sydney Airport, which followed a heart-wrenching and tearful departure where about 150 close friends came to bid use farewell and see us off.

I was fifty years old and at an age when most men are thinking about retirement; and here I was starting all over again from scratch, with barely anything and knowing hardly anybody in the Northeast!

My second son, David, who was 14 at the time, remarked a little later that his first impression of America was the smoke stacks of Newark as we drove down the New Jersey Turnpike for the first time. He thought all America was like this. No wonder New Jersey gets such a bad rap!

Shortly before leaving Australia, a visiting American pastor and friend remarked, when he found out we were moving to America, "Well I can understand you wanting to go to America, but New Jersey – that's got to be God!"

We were picked up by our close friends, Gary and Cindy Panepinto, who were the executive pastor and associate pastor respectively at The Church of Grace and Peace at the time. We stayed at their place for the first few days until the house the church had arranged for us to live in was ready.

This house had been empty for a number of years and volunteers from the church filled about 10 trucks with trash and junk that was cleared out from the property. By the time we moved in, church members had provided everything from furniture, crockery and cutlery to appliances. The only things we needed to buy were our beds.

We lived in that house rent-free for a year until we bought our own place and moved in a year later, to the day, from when we arrived.

Two kind folks each provided a vehicle for us to use free of charge for the first year, covering all costs like insurance and registration.

Clearly, God was using the tremendous generosity of the American people to make provision for His vision for us – if it's His will, it's His bill!

Fish Out of Water

We all felt like fish out of water for a long time. We had come from an outdoor to an indoor culture. It's one thing to visit a place; it's another thing altogether to live there. Guests are afforded a lot of 'grace,' but immigrants are expected to fit right in!

Culture is mostly unwritten. Nobody gives you a cultural rule book when you arrive in a new country. Most of the time, you have to learn by trial and error. And that can be rather painful!

Australia has a very 'no frills' culture. What you see is what you get! That can be very intimidating to Americans who go there, because they come from an affirmation culture where kids are taught from 'knee-high' to always make an effort to be nice, polite and kind to people, even if you don't like them. The 'glass half full' view of this is that it can take a lot of effort, discipline and can be quite noble. The glass 'half empty' view is that it can come across as insincere to Australians because of their high appreciation of honesty, no matter what. You will always know where you stand with an Australian.

Going Native?

I was beginning to negotiate my third culture and now the shoe was on the other foot! Culture shock usually takes the form of two extremes – people either go 'native,' becoming almost a caricature of the original, or they become very cynical toward their adopted culture, never seeing anything positive about it and always making comparisons with how good it was where they came from.

It's all about expectations, unrealistic or unrealized! Because of our closeness as cultures, Americans tend to think that Australians think like them, and vice versa. Just because we all speak English in New Zealand, Australia and America doesn't mean the culture is the same!

If I was to have an interaction with someone from Japan for instance, I would have far fewer expectations of common ground due to the vast differences between western and eastern cultures and therefore, less potential for conflict.

But when cultures are close, there is a ripe environment for trouble. That's why civil wars are the most vicious of wars!

I think I lost count of the times I stumbled and bumbled my way through the first couple of years in the USA. My Aussie directness was just too much for this culture; it's a wonder I made any friends at all! But in spite of me, God did speak to a few leaders, telling them to embrace me. One of those leaders was Joe Mattera.

Bosom Buddies with a Boy from Brooklyn

I had become friends with Tommy Tenney after he visited Australia a couple of times just prior to our leaving. Tommy advised me to make contact with Joe as soon as I got to America. He said Pastor Mattera might not have the biggest church in New York City, but he certainly had a lot of influence.

My first meeting with Joe Mattera was for lunch at a Brooklyn Diner. We immediately hit it off and fast became friends as I shared with him about my background and why we had come to America. Joe invited me to preach at his church a few months later, and it was obvious we shared a similar vision.

Shortly after that, Joe called a meeting of some of his friends and associates in ministry, including me. His purpose for the meeting was the formation of a new apostolic network in the greater Metro New York Area, which includes New Jersey and Connecticut. The network, City Covenant Coalition (CCC), was founded in November 1999.

At our second meeting a few weeks later, Joe and founding executive member, Bishop Roderick Caesar from

Jamaica, Queens asked me to be Chairman of the CCC Leadership Committee. I told them I was honored with the offer, but questioned whether the other leaders would accept me in this position, being the 'new kid on the block,' so to speak. Most did, a few did not – mainly because of cultural differences.

Bishop Caesar's first question to me when we met the first time was, "So, how long are you going to be here?" As one of the city's spiritual fathers, his question was predicated by a plethora of ministries in the city... ministries that had come and gone... each with a vision to 'take the city for Jesus' – a fact that was a frustration to those like him whose entire lives and ministries had been spent working the hard, dry spiritual ground of the Northeast. I told him I had no plans of leaving this side of heaven!

Besides, we are never called to take a city, but to serve it!

In the **Shadow** of **Eternity!**

CHAPTER 10
Re-establishing Ministry

Putting Some Roots Down

Just prior to our arrival, Pastor Healy had asked two precious ladies from the church, Yvonne Doval and Maryann Goyette, to make calls to pastors on our behalf to arrange ministry engagements for me when I arrived. Despite the tyranny of never getting a human on the line, they persisted and had some degree of success. My first staff in America consisted of Yvonne and Maryann; they worked for FMI for many years.

Very quickly, I set my hand to the task of submitting my vision to as many pastors and leaders in the Northeast as possible. I knew I would need to work with my nose to the grindstone for the first few years to get established in ministry in America, and I knew that would only flow out of relationship.

The irony for me was that I had been used to getting on jets every week to minister, and now I was driving up and down the Garden State Parkway and New Jersey Turnpike! Being in a different nation every month was normal for me. Now I was restricted to a metroplex that contained 70 million people and stretched from Boston to Washington, DC, and out to Pittsburg, Pennsylvania! The Lord did, however, encourage me about that.

The Strategic Metron

Without question, the Northeast of America is perhaps one of the world's most strategic areas. The center of world economy is still Wall Street in New York City. And even though we are pretty much entrenched in a world economy, if Wall Street sneezes, the rest of the world catches a cold!

The center of world media is there, too. The movies may be made in Hollywood, but the scripts are written in NYC! And we should never underestimate the power and influence of American popular culture expressed through movies and television.

The center of world military and political power is in the Pentagon and the White House in Washington, DC. And we dare not forget all the Ivy League colleges and universities like Yale and Harvard, just to mention a few, which are not only training up the future leaders of this nation, but just about every other nation in the world that sends their young people to the Northeast for higher education... if we can call it that. Any impact on this area will filter out to the rest of America and eventually touch the whole world!

The Shock of the First Winter

Toward the end of 1999, some small progress was being made in establishing my ministry. I would drive all day long, there and back, just to have lunch with a pastor and share my vision and the passion that led us to the Northeast.

We were also about to experience our first Northeastern winter. This was to be an education for us, having come from a climate in Australia where it was 'beautiful one day, perfect the next!' Snow and ice were a novelty to us, and I was about to learn the hard way.

Early in January, I walked out the back door of our home, wearing leather-soled shoes, totally unaware of the ice on the steps. My feet suddenly shot out in front of me so that I was almost perpendicular with the ground for an instant... then I crashed down, hitting the sharp edge of the step with the full force of my weight at the middle of my back. I instantly went into shock, stood up and managed to stumble back in through the doorway, only to then collapse onto the floor as if a thousand knives were thrust into my back. The pain was excruciating!

I lay face down, unable to move and thinking I had broken my back, until some friends... and my chiropractor... rushed over and tried to get me up on my feet. Needless to say, that was not happening! Every time they tried to move me, the thousand knives dug deeper. I spent the next 10 days on my stomach on the floor of our living room, unable to move. My back was not broken, but it was severely bruised internally. However, it was during this time that I heard from God! It's an ill wind that doesn't blow some good!

CHAPTER 11
The Vision of the Great Wheel of Reawakening

We had been so consumed with just getting to the Northeast from the other side of the world that what I was supposed to do when I got here was not all that clear. To find out would take a different kind of grace! While I was on the floor and soon afterward, God began to crystallize a vision in my heart. Following is what I recorded on our website (www.firepowerint.com) on February 18, 2000.

The Coming Wheel of Re-awakening –
A Prophetic Word for the Northeast of America

95

The Big Wet and the Big Dry

In the far northwest of Australia, in the hottest and most remote part of the outback, it can get up to 110 degrees in the shade. Nothing much lives there other than a few snakes, lizards and crocodiles. There are only two seasons – the "Big Wet" and the "Big Dry" – as they are called in that part of Australia.

The wet season hits around December or January and brings torrential "monsoon" rains. These may last for a couple of months, but then there is virtually no rain for the rest of the year. It just gets drier and drier until December, the hottest and driest month, comes again. At that time, once lush rivers have almost dried up and fish can be seen flopping around in the mud. Sometimes the crocodiles are left to fight over the last few flopping fish in dried up lake beds.

If you had ears that could hear creation speak, you would hear a desperate cry to the heavens to send the reviving rain again or all would soon perish.

Then something interesting happens. Just before the rains come again, a thick band of humidity pushes down ahead of them from the tropical north. If it was unbearably hot before, now it was extremely uncomfortable, as well! But then shortly afterward, the life-giving rains come and all nature breathes a sigh of relief.

However, because the land is largely flat and compacted from the long period of dryness, it does not readily absorb the torrents of water – flash floods are very common. Ground-dwelling creatures have learned that the very thing that will revive them can also drown them. Many have learned they must go up (into trees) or down (burrow into the earth) lest they get swept away!

96

I believe this picture can provide us with some insight into the current spiritual state of the Northeast of America! Many have felt that the spiritual environment in the Northeast is hot and dry and have cried out in desperation to God to send the rains of revival. The humidity has been too much for some, and they have given up. But God would have us endure because a new season of spiritual lushness will soon come as a result of the fresh rains.

Whatever you do, don't be found on middle ground when the rains come, or else the very thing that could save you might sweep you away. It's better to be hot or cold than to be lukewarm!

I believe with all my heart that God will visit the Northeast in our lifetime. Will it be overnight? Probably not! In my experience, the Kingdom of God is built piece by piece, line by line, precept upon precept, by faithful men and women who have His vision for their area deeply branded in their hearts and who have covenanted with others of like spirit and similar vision to see it come to pass. As John 13:35 declares: "By this all will know that you are My disciples, if you have love for one another."

The Nazareth Stigma

I believe the Spirit of the Lord would have us know that He is the One who has allowed the Northeast of America to become, as its reputation says, a hard, dry spiritual place. Not that He issued orders for this to be, more that He permitted it to happen in much the same way He permitted Job to be tested.

He has allowed a "Nazareth Stigma" to arise over this area! The byword spoken by many major and well-intentioned ministries has been, "Can any good thing come out of the Northeast?" And therefore, most of their efforts have been focused in other areas of America and the world... areas considered to be more 'fruitful.'

"It has been My purpose to allow this place to become barren even though it was once a prosperous land spiritually. For I am about to visit this place again! When I do, no man will be able to claim the glory because they have avoided the Northeast like the plague, for there was no obvious fruit to be seen.

But the fruit that I have been nurturing is only visible to spiritual eyes and is watered from a deep longing in the souls of a few desperate, faithful saints who have cried out to Me continually. I have stood by and watched their hunger grow in the dry, dark places as the enemy of their souls has done his worst to take them from Me. But I have watched over them as a shepherd stands guard over his flock and protected them when the wolf came to rob, kill and destroy.

The time has come! My visitation will not come by a man's method or strategy, but by My Spirit."

The Vision of the Big Wheel

I saw a vision of a giant wheel towering above the land and everything in it. It was rolling slowly into the Northeast of America. This wheel had many teeth around its outer rim, like the teeth of a clock's internal gears. There were four thick spokes joining the outer rim to the hub. God showed me that this huge structure represented the Coming Wheel of Reawakening!

The teeth on the wheel represented all the ministries that have heard the call and, in obedience, have already or soon will, relocate to the Northeast. Among the teeth were also many ministries from this area, which are being sharpened and prepared.

The four thick spokes represented four ingredients that are the fruits of hunger and dryness – PRAYER, PURPOSE, POWER AND PASSION. The hub they were attached to and revolving around was called UNITY! Every ingredient of this giant wheel was integrated and interdependent.

PRAYER to capture the attention of God!
PURPOSE attained from hearing His heart!
POWER to enable the outworking of His purposes!
PASSION to move us out from apathy to activity!
UNITY to counteract the Spirit of Independence!

As I watched the Big Wheel turn, the teeth on the outer rim were plowing up the hard, dry ground of the Northeast of America, preparing it for new seed and for the rains soon to come.

Lord, let the wheel roll!" (February 18, 2000)

In the **Shadow** of **Eternity!**

CHAPTER 12
Getting a Foothold and 9/11!

The Church that Dripped Oil!

I met Pastor Don James on one of my visits prior to moving here and we became fast friends as he sought encouragement from a neutral source about some ministry matters.

After we relocated here, he invited me to minister on a Friday night at Bethany Church, where he pastored in Wyckoff, New Jersey. It was a powerful meeting! Toward the end, I asked Don to join me as I anointed the altar generously with oil and prayed that the Lord would visit us mightily. I then invited folks up to the front for healing.

After I had been ministering for some time, out of the corner of my eye, I noticed people were gathering under a set of doors on the left side of the stage. They were reaching up and wiping their fingers on the doorpost. They then came over to show us what appeared to be sweet-smelling oil on their fingers. As much as they wiped it off the doorpost, it kept coming back. The door on the other side of the stage began to manifest the same phenomenon, and then the rafters in the ceiling did the same. It was a clear supernatural answer to our prayer!

Shortly afterward, Charisma magazine did an article on our mission in the Northeast and included a report on the church that dripped oil. Pastor Don is now the Assistant Presbyter for the Assemblies of God in New Jersey and we have remained close friends to this day.

Making an Imprint on the Region and 9/11

During the first four years we were in America, I worked diligently in my own ministry and through City Covenant Coalition (CCC) to begin to have an impact on the Northeast.

However, things all changed instantly on the morning of September 11, 2001. I no sooner pulled out of the driveway on my way to the office than my daughter, Rebekah, called. She had just seen a news flash on TV reporting that a small plane had hit one of the Twin Towers of the World Trade Center!

This was the start of a day that would dramatically alter the course of the history of the world forever!

By late morning, the Twin Towers had fallen and 3,000 people had perished in the first real attack to take place on American soil.

In the months that followed, the Church responded to the tragedy through the efforts of the Northeast Clergy Group, led by Pastors Rick Del Rio and Marcus Rivera and comprised mainly of churches and ministries in the area of Ground Zero and throughout the city. CCC became a part of this broad group, having lost many members from churches affiliated with us.

Over the next year, we all pulled together in the clean up and relief efforts.

New York's Finest – Rev. John Picarello 9/11 Testimony

Pastor John Picarello is a founding member of CCC and pastors a church on Staten Island. He is also a veteran of many years service as a New York fire fighter. On the morning of 9/11, soon after the second plane hit the South Tower, his unit was called into lower Manhattan to help with the rescue efforts.

Pastor and FDNY fireman John Picarello

Here is his testimony in his own words:

A First Hand Account of the Collapse of the World Trade Center by Reverend John S. Picarello

"The morning of Tuesday, September 11, 2001 was a beautiful spring-like morning in New York City. I had gone to work, which for me was a morning just like any other, leaving home early to get in ahead of the morning rush hour traffic. My firehouse was located in the Sunset Park section of Brooklyn, housing Engine Company 278 and the 40th Battalion, to which I was assigned.

Sitting around the kitchen table, we were all engaged in conversation, which was usual at the morning change of tours, when our attention was drawn to the pictures being broadcast on the morning news. We have just learned that a plane had slammed into the North Tower of the World Trade Center (also known as Tower One); it was now approximately 8:46am.

A second alarm was transmitted and then a third alarm shortly thereafter. At 8:54am, Battalion 40 was assigned to respond to a staging area on the Brooklyn side of the Battery Tunnel. On this particular tour, I was working with Battalion Chief Edward Henry, who at that time had some 40 years of experience on the job.

As we headed down 4th Avenue for the Battery Tunnel, we could see the upper floors of the North Tower engulfed in flames and huge billows of smoke rising high into the sky. At first we thought the plane had accidentally hit the North Tower as a plane had once hit the Empire State Building many years ago; we thought nothing more of it until a few minutes later.

It was now just a few minutes past 9:00am and we were approaching the Tunnel when the second plane struck the South Tower. It was at this time that Chief Henry and I looked at each other and said, "Terrorists!" We now knew that this was no accident. Immediately, all units were ordered to continue to respond on the scene. It was a bit difficult getting through the tunnel, as it was jammed with vehicles. An open lane was eventually established for emergency vehicles coming into the city.

Arriving on the scene, I was awed at the magnitude of destruction caused by the airliners. Both towers had sustained heavy damage, with several floors now fully engulfed in flames. The streets were littered with debris falling from the towers. I was sick to my stomach, watching in horror as people leapt from the upper floors. I remember trying to come to grips with the reality of what I was seeing, realizing that this was no movie; it was actually happening.

I have no words to adequately describe the scene I was witnessing. My eyes began to fill up as I prayed for the people as they fell; it seemed to take forever. Some were holding hands, two and three at a time were coming down. I can't even begin to imagine those last moments on the upper floors and the conditions those people must have faced before feeling compelled to make such a decision. I prayed for their families with the sobering understanding that I was seeing the final moments of their lives.

Chief Henry had entered the lobby of the Marriott Hotel situated at the foot of both towers; I followed a few moments later. The lobby was a staging area where units were receiving their assignments; we were assigned to go to the 75th floor of the North Tower (Tower One). There were many firefighters, police and emergency personnel present in the lobby by this time.

Upon receiving our assignments, a group of us began to make our way through the lobby toward Tower One. We had only walked a few feet when we heard a rumbling sound in the distance; it was coming from outside and seemed to be getting closer. A few seconds later, the floor began to vibrate as the entire lobby started shaking. The rumbling was like a huge freight train coming closer; it sounded as if it were all around us. We all headed for shelter.

Some of us dove onto the floor toward an interior wall and covered up as best we could. I had only run a few steps when everything came violently crashing down around us. The sound was deafening, then in a matter of seconds, it was over. Everything was completely dark and quiet; blanketed by an eerie silence.

I remember landing on top of Safety Battalion Chief Lawrence Stack who was in front of me at the time of the collapse. I had my hands on his back when everything came crashing down. The ceilings had collapsed on both sides of us. We didn't know it at the time, but the hotel had just taken a direct hit from the collapse of the South Tower (Tower Two). I was on the floor and remember praying. I had just enough time to call on the name of Jesus a second before everything went black.

It seemed like an eternity when, in fact, it was just a few seconds. When I opened my eyes, everything was pitch black. I realized I was not pinned under any debris. To my left just a few feet away, there was nothing but twisted steel and rubble from one end of the room to the other. The wall we were leaning against had shifted, pinning the edge of Chief Stack's turnout coat to the ground. He had to slip out of it before he could stand up. To our right were two firefighters, trapped from the waist down in what appeared to be a wall of debris.

I worked with a few others to help dig them out, and they were free in a short time. As we looked around, we could tell we were cut off from the rest of the lobby by a wall of debris. A large area had collapsed just a few feet behind me. We were cut off from the exits in front of us and behind us, so we were now trapped in the lobby.

Chief Henry began to call outside on his radio, but there was no response. It wasn't until later that the significance of no one responding to our radio transmissions dawned on me. At this point, there were about nine, maybe 10, of us together, as well as some hotel guests and personnel. I did not know what had happened to the other emergency personnel I saw in the lobby area earlier, many of whom were friends.

We then began to look for a way out of the hotel. Although it was still pitch black, I could see some fires burning through the openings in the debris not far from us. We felt a slight breeze coming from the front of the lobby and followed it, eventually making our way to an area where we found three doors. One door led to a stairway to a lower level, which we did not take because some of the people with us had serious injuries. Another door opened to a long corridor that led to an opening on West Street. It's hard to describe what West Street looked like; so much of it appeared to be destroyed, and the debris was deep enough to cover the pavement.

It was there I saw the Department Chief Peter Ganci, standing in the center of West Street looking up at the debris still falling. He had come from the Command Post and there was nothing but rubble all around him.

We were at an opening with a knee wall about four feet high. He began waving to us to make our way out of the building. One firefighter at a time would go over the wall and head outside. As the Chief would wave them on, they ran past him to the other side of the street. A couple of firefighters headed out before me, and there were still some people with us who were injured and couldn't get over that wall.

Chief Henry had gone to my right looking for another way out before I arrived at that opening with the others. Chief Ganci motioned to me to come out; at first, I was going to stay and help the others, but he kept motioning for me to come over to him, so I did. He ordered me to go find the Command Post, which was being repositioned north of Vesey Street due to the collapse of Tower Two. He was requesting four more ladder companies, a squad company and a rescue company, if one was available. They were to report to him as soon as possible. That was the last time I would see him alive.

In front of Tower One, I was passing under the walkway known as the North Bridge that crosses over West Street. I stopped momentarily to catch my breath and, had it not been for the Chief's order, I'd have sat there a few minutes. About this time, I once again began to hear a rumbling sound. Looking up, I saw the huge spire atop Tower One start to sway; over my shoulder, Tower One began to collapse. The rumbling got louder and the ground started to shake. The Tower began to pancake, making very loud crumbling sounds... bap, bap, bap, bap... as each floor collapsed upon the others. I saw flashes of fire and debris being forced away from the building as it started to come down; it appeared to be coming right at me.

The thought crossed my mind, "This is not a dream you'll wake up from; this is real, you've got to run!" The thought so resonated within me that I felt as though I was being pulled across the street. I started to run, but my legs felt like jelly and I had a feeling I couldn't run fast enough. The fear that came over me was extreme and lasted only a second or two before my feelings went numb. I was still in full bunker gear with my air pack on my back, and I was already exhausted from the first collapse.

I began feeling a pressure on my back when, from the corner of my eye, I saw everything start to go gray and get darker. Once across West and Vesey Streets, I dove behind a truck and everything blew past me like a hurricane of debris and thick black smoke. It was like the roar of a tornado as things fell all over the place; the truck was rocking from the wind and debris hitting it. I just covered my head and prayed!

I remember reminding God from the 23rd Psalm, "You promised that when we walked through the valley of the shadow of death... Oh Lord, You promised." It seemed like such a long time, but again, it was probably just a few moments and then everything went black once more, and there was another eerie silence… a stillness in the air so quiet I heard nothing. Dead silence. When I opened my eyes I could see nothing, it was like still having my eyes closed; everything around me was pitch black. Looking up, I couldn't see the sun, the sky or anything but darkness for a moment or two.

I took a breath and the air was solid; it was like breathing sawdust. As the smoke began to clear, I managed to stumble to my feet. Every two or three steps I would fall back down again. I was coughing and spitting up what seemed like small rocks and dirt and trying to clean out my eyes. I couldn't use my face piece because it was impacted with dirt. The only radio transmission I heard at this time was from Chief Henry, checking on me and letting me know he was okay and had gotten out. Later, we would discover that only a few of us, of the ten or more trapped together in the lobby, had survived the collapse of Tower One.

Once the smoke began to lift, I could see the magnitude of the destruction. It was immense! Standing at the corner of West Street and Vesey, I could see fires everywhere. Debris more than three or four stories high stretched for blocks. The North Bridge, where I had stopped to catch my breath just minutes before, was crushed to the ground. It was acting like a dam, preventing tons of debris from rolling across Vesey Street. The scene was too much for my mind to process at one time.

I remained on the scene working until early afternoon, when I found an ambulance and asked to be looked at. I was then taken to an uptown hospital to be treated and was able to call my wife to let her know I was alright. After some tests, I was released and returned to the scene around 4:00pm. I worked until I was too exhausted to work any longer; that was about 8:30pm.

I thought of how God had spared me in the midst of all this destruction and there was not a scratch on me, not a scratch. When I finally arrived home around midnight, I asked my wife how she managed to deal with the events of that day, knowing I was there and not hearing from me until late in the afternoon. She said that as she prayed, the Lord reminded her of a prophetic word that we had both received at a Pastor's Meeting a few years earlier. The man giving the word to us turned to her and said, "I see a truck; I don't know what that means, but Elena, this is for you. The Lord does not want you to be afraid when your husband goes to work. The devil has tried to take his life before, but he will not be snatched away from you. God will protect him, and He wants you to know that."

My wife said to me, "Imagine how much God cares about how I feel that He would give me that word knowing I would need it to hold onto in the future!" I am grateful and comforted that even in the midst of chaos, when we cannot understand what is happening or how things will go for us, God is still in control.

In time, I would learn about those who were trapped with us by the collapse of Tower Two and who had not survived the collapse of Tower One. I had lost 24 friends and 343 brothers in the fire department. Among them was a long time friend from grammar school, Lieutenant Phillip Petti, who had given his life when returning to the upper floors of the hotel in a rescue attempt as Tower One collapsed. Chief Edward Henry lost his youngest son, Firefighter Joseph Henry of Ladder 21, who had served less than a year. Battalion Chief Lawrence Stack was in the process of helping others when he was caught in the collapse of Tower One.

In the year following that tragic day, my family and I would become well acquainted with the effects of Post Traumatic Stress and its impact on people. Facing the reality of our own mortality and emotions such as fear, insecurity and anger would have to be addressed. Along with the support of others, God revealed Himself to us in so many ways as The Great Physician during that period.

I witnessed the pain and suffering so many would have to endure in losing loved ones that day. Seeing this throughout the seemingly endless funerals and memorials that followed September 2001, I longed for more of the grace of God Paul describes in 2 Corinthians 1:3-4, "...the Father of mercies and God of all comfort, Who comforts us in all our affliction, so that we may be able to comfort those who are in any affliction, with the comfort with which we ourselves are comforted by God."

This experience brought about a profound change in my life and ministry. I could have searched for deeper theological understanding of God's sovereignty and His Divine providential actions in such tragedies, but my heart cried out more for His healing of the masses instead. I longed for Him to show me how to minister His healing love to others the way He had so graciously ministered to me.

Three Hundred Forty Three firefighters made the ultimate sacrifice on September 11, 2001. That day, Police, Fire, EMS, Port Authority, and a host of others formed the largest combined rescue effort in American history up to that time.

Please remember to pray for the rescue workers who serve in your community."

In the 'Garden'

On the first anniversary of 9/11, along with the Northeast Clergy Group, CCC co-sponsored a concert at Madison Square Garden in midtown Manhattan. Top-line Christian groups and artists, including Third Day, Toby Mac, and many others volunteered their time and talents as a tribute that day.

The 'Garden' was packed, as the memory of 9/11 was still fresh and heavy on most people's hearts. John Picarello shared his testimony that night.

Jeff with Toby Mac at "Madison Square Garden" on the first anniversary of 911

CHAPTER 13
Championing Traditional Marriage in the Northeast

C CC's influence dramatically increased when we spearheaded a campaign to defend traditional marriage after several attempts to redefine it in New York State.

This culminated in several key events that galvanized the church around a cause to a level of unity that crossed most denominational boundaries. The first was the CCC sponsored Defense of Marriage Clergy Press Conference on the steps of New York's City Hall on Monday, March 29, 2004.

It was the largest gathering of clergy for an event of this type in the history of the city, rallying strong and equal representation from all ethnic and religious groups.

Second was the huge Renewal of Vows for Traditional Marriage Rally, where 2,500 couples gathered on Broadway on July 25, 2004 to renew their wedding vows that hot Sunday afternoon. Fellow CCC member, Reverend Victor Nazario and I co-chaired this event. The city allowed us to cordon off several blocks along Broadway for the Rally. On stage, we had a representation of most of the city's spiritual fathers.

Challenging Mayor Bloomberg in New York City Hall

These events were well covered by the media and eventually got the attention of Mayor Bloomberg, who was about to run for his second term at that time. Consequently, the leaders of CCC were invited to meet with him in his office at City Hall.

Before being elected mayor, Bloomberg was chairman of a giant multi-national corporation named after him; he had become a multi-billionaire as a result. Mayor Bloomberg was a very astute Jewish businessman, who had originally run for mayor on the Republican ticket. However, this was mere pragmatic politics because at heart he was a libertarian.

We all gathered one Wednesday morning at 10am and went through the enhanced security brought on by 9/11, then were ushered into the mayor's office, which was not what you would have expected. His desk was at the center of a huge room, with about 150 other desks and cubicles in concentric circles working out from his. In the front of this open hall was a reception area and café for guests, which we were ushered into.

Largest ever New Jersey Clergy Press Conference in Defense of Traditional Marriage on the steps of the Capital in Trenton

He had equipped all the surrounding individual offices with glass walls and doors. His reasoning behind this, he told us a little later, was that a lot of bad stuff goes on "behind closed doors!" He was very particular about having a transparent administration.

About eight of us from CCC sat down at a large conference table in the reception area and were served light refreshments from the café as we began a dialogue with the Mayor.

His interest in us was obvious! We had a lot of influence over the church within the city and he was running for a second term. He needed our support.

As we talked and began to feel each other out, the conversation eventually landed on traditional marriage and gay marriage. Bloomberg finally said that he was not

115

opposed to anyone getting married if they loved each other, but would be personally opposed if one of his daughters came home one day and said she wanted to marry a girl!

I responded to his comments by saying, "With great respect, Mister Mayor, we are more concerned with the macro view rather than the micro view! Since the beginning of humanity, including the foundation of every major religion, marriage has always been defined as between a woman and a man. It has been passed on this way through every generation in human history, with an expectation that we should present it to those coming after us as something better, not worse! We think it is the height of arrogance for our generation to think we have the right to redefine and water down what has always been the basic component of a continuing and prospering society."

His answer was, "Well, I'd like to meet with you another time to talk more about that," which I interpreted as meaning, "I don't have an answer!"

We finished our discussion, clearly letting him know where we stood on certain issues. He was very warm and gracious to us.

As we continued our meeting on a more social basis, a youngish woman came over and started a conversation with me. We talked about a number of issues and why we were there that day. Finally, after having a very pleasant chat for about five minutes, I said, "Well, my name is Jeff Beacham, and you are?" She replied, "I'm Caroline Kennedy." I had not recognized the last remaining child of President John F. Kennedy and greatly embarrassed, replied, "Oh dear, please forgive me; I'm just an ignorant Australian. I should have realized."

Simultaneously, one of the CCC members who had come over to observe the conversation, walked away partly embarrassed and partly disgusted that I had no idea who she was. "Ahh, Jeff!" he exclaimed in frustration. But to be honest, I've had to rely on Australian ignorance several times to get out of some tight spots!

In the **Shadow** of **Eternity!**

CHAPTER 14
Marriage Breakdown

Taking Its Toll!

By early 2003, we had toiled hard for nearly four years to get established in the Northeast.

Being transplanted into a whole new ministry culture had been enormously challenging and required a season of almost total dedication, entailing long hours in the office and on the road, sometimes traveling all day just to have lunch with a pastor to share my vision and hopefully begin a relationship that would eventually result in fruitful ministry.

After four years, I was beginning to see some fruit develop when suddenly everything changed!

I had left home life and the children primarily in the hands of my wife and, despite enormous challenges of a different kind for her and our children as a result of the transition, there did seem to be some bright spots.

These included owning our first house ever here in New Jersey, something that had always eluded us with Sydney's sky high prices, and the Lord was taking care of all our transportation needs for the family and ministry.

One of the challenges for me was adjusting from an Australian ministry base that entailed air travel to a different nation an average of once a month and flying around Australia the rest of the time, to driving almost everywhere for ministry... up and down the Garden State Parkway and New Jersey Turnpike!

However, one of our biggest challenges as a family was coming from a very relational culture like Australia to a more task-oriented one here in America. We really missed our 'mates!'

The Shock of the High Price

Early in 2003, my former wife, Heather came to me saying she would like to make a trip to New Zealand, where we were both born and raised, to catch up with everybody.

Although friends and family had visited us in Australia every year or so during the time leading up to our relocation to America, she had not been home in seven years and missed everything and everyone. I understood that and didn't have a problem with her going. So, a few weeks later she made the long and arduous journey 'down under.'

While she was there, she was able to catch up with both sides of the family and had apparently given positive reports of our progress adjusting to life in America. However, at some point toward the end of that trip, something drastically changed!

Within 24 hours of returning, my wife announced that she was going to leave America and relocate back home to live in New Zealand!

After trying to contain my initial shock, my first response to her was, "But we both were assured beyond a doubt that it was God's will for us to come to America!" Her answer was, "I just can't pay the price anymore!" And it had been a very high price to pay indeed, for all of us, but especially for her.

Counting the Cost

In the year prior to our relocation, we had tried to work through every possible scenario of how the decision to move to America might affect our family.

What would happen if any of our kids eventually wanted to move back to Australia? What would happen if we moved back, and they wanted to stay? There were any number of possibilities and we felt we had covered them all, but I had never considered divorce!

The months that followed were the worst to endure.

At first, I thought it was a serious case of home sickness, which had sometimes happened previously after returning from visits to New Zealand while we were still living in Australia. They would usually last about a week, then life would slowly return to normal. A week passed, and Heather grew even more resolute.

I saw then that this could be serious and we'd need to take it to the FMI Board first. After hearing from both of us, the Board's initial response was that there was nothing involved requiring such drastic action. They suggested we have a break for a month or so, undergo counseling from an independent source and then reassess the situation.

However, it seemed nothing could deter this course of action, and I watched as my whole world, built around family, faith and ministry began to fall apart.

Not long after this issue began, I told Heather that for the sake of keeping the family together at all costs, I would be prepared to give up everything here in the Northeast and relocate to New Zealand with her. She informed me that I could move 'down under' if I wanted to, but I would not be living with her.

There were no moral issues on my part; neither were there financial nor other issues that traditionally cause family and ministry downfalls. But in May that year, my wife left for New Zealand with three of our five children.

I found myself alone, night after night, in a house that had just a short time ago been a vibrant home full of life and activity. The loneliness was appalling! The shock was devastating!

Ministry Survival!

The Board of FMI determined that we would not let this get 'swept under the carpet,' as has happened in many situations, but that we would bring it to the light.

We compiled a list of about 120 key leaders specifically from the Northeast, and others from around the world with whom I had close relationships, and sent a series of letters to inform them of these tragic developments.

The first letter included a statement from Pastor Walt Healy (FMI Board member and pastor of The Church of Grace and Peace, our home base) outlining the situation, one from me, and another from my wife, explaining the situation and encouraging people to still have faith in the vision God had shown me for the Northeast.

There were only two negative responses from all the letters we sent, including the follow ups we subsequently sent out over the next year. Some pastors even remarked that they were going to keep those letters as a reference on how to deal with such issues.

Eventually, the ministry survived; although the family suffered tremendously, which is certainly not the way it should be, and the repercussions are still going on today. The cost has indeed been high!

One ministry friend remarked, "God gives the call and He anoints it, but people always have to walk it out in their humanity!"

Regrouping and Rebuilding

As I began to regroup, I knew I would need to rebuild a lot of support to protect my personal and ministry life from that point onward.

I surrounded myself with strong accountability, both personally and in the ministry, and made sure I was beyond moral reproach, never being alone with a woman. Several female members of the FMI Board kept an eye on my back wherever we went together for conferences and events and, shall we say, they did an excellent job!

As a very social person, I was racked with loneliness, something I had not experienced throughout our entire 23 years of marriage, but now I was languishing!

However, many great families and individuals from our local church gathered around and I was able to build a healthy social network, which was a life saver, and those relationships remain some of my closest to this day!

At the end of 2003, some close ministry associates gathered together and helped finance a trip to New Zealand so I could go try to bring about reconciliation between my estranged wife and myself. Unfortunately however, it was to no avail.

Sadly, after two years, I had no choice but to acquiesce to New Zealand's two year divorce law and it became final.

Heather had moved on with her life and was married shortly thereafter.

CHAPTER 15
Remarriage

Meeting Melva

Toward the end of 2003, I attended a conference in Dallas, Texas and was invited to a private function on one of the free nights. This get together was to gather some key leaders from around the nation to discuss their potential involvement in a marketplace ministry project.

As I walked into the room, I recognized just about everyone there, other than one woman sitting opposite me. The meeting went well and at the conclusion, since she was the only person there I didn't know, I introduced myself.

"I'm Melva Lea!" she responded. Still a relative newcomer to the American Charismatic community, that did not immediately click for me. Observing my 'still-don't-know-any-better' expression that had gotten the better of me when I met Caroline Kennedy, Melva felt the need to expand a little bit. "I was previously married to Larry Lea," she added. And once again, I pleaded the 'Aussie' ignorance excuse!

Larry and Melva had been used by God to raise up a Prayer Army, nationally and internationally – 370,000 in America alone – based on the revelation he had been given on the Lord's Prayer. Larry would later be accredited with being a major pioneer in the modern worldwide prayer movement!

In the Eighties and Nineties, they pastored the fastest growing church in America, Church on the Rock in Rockwall, Texas, which had an auditorium that could seat over 5,000. Regrettably, against her wishes Melva and Larry divorced in 1999.

Vulnerability

The next day, I ran into Melva between sessions and decided to ask her how she handled what she had been through, revealing that I was going through a similar situation. She responded, "Well, you're very vulnerable right now and should put people all around you who can protect you from yourself and others, especially emotionally!" After our brief discussion, I thanked her for her encouragement, knowing that I had already begun implementing some of her suggestions.

I never saw Melva again until the following year, when I attended the same annual conference again. In any case, I was still married, even if separated, wearing my wedding ring, and holding onto the prospect of reconciliation, no matter how remote. We enjoyed some polite conversation, but that was it.

Getting Serious

However, a lot had happened by the time I got back to the conference a year later in 2005. The divorce had been finalized, and my close counselors and Board all felt there was no reason why I should not be open to the prospect of a new relationship, should one ever arise.

At the conference, Melva and I, being practically the only 'single' people there, sat together for a few sessions, under the watchful eye of my 'minders.' On the last day, we had lunch together in the restaurant of the hotel where the event was held; and all eyes were on us there!

During lunch, we shared our visions for ministry and more about our history and decided it would be good to stay in touch. However, Melva remarked, "Well, my Mama always told me that girls don't call boys," to which I told her I would be happy to call her.

After lunch, we both shared a shuttle to the nearby Dallas airport, where I was flying back to New Jersey and she was off to another city to preach for the weekend. So, waiting at our separate gates, I decided right then and there to call her! She seemed pleasantly surprised. We exchanged some more pleasantries, wished each other well and committed to speak again soon.

Over December 2005 and January 2006, we spoke a few times by phone and realized we could meet briefly at JFK Airport in January when Melva was on a layover awaiting a connecting flight to Israel. So I drove up from New Jersey to JFK and met her there.

We were so excited to see each other that night that after she left to board her flight and I was on my way out of the airport, I got a call from Melva to say she had missed her flight! Needless to say, I turned around and found her again! We were able to confirm another flight for three hours later, which meant we were able to spend some additional quality time together.

Later, as she was about to go through security, I dutifully put my arm around her and prayed a prayer of protection for the long Atlantic flight, said goodbye and kissed her on the cheek as she began to leave. And then I grabbed her arm, pulled her close to me and kissed her again – this time on the mouth! Melva later commented, "That did it for me!"

A month later, Melva flew into New Jersey for the weekend to be the guest speaker at our home base, The Church of Grace and Peace. And guess who was assigned to drive her around?

Well, between a long distance relationship (Melva was living in Jerusalem at the time) and periodic visits to New Jersey, we were engaged in April and married in November of 2006.

We had a wonderful honeymoon in Cancun, after which we began not just a marriage, but a merging of ministries. Then, a little over two years later, we got news we didn't want to hear!

CHAPTER 16
Cancer

Discovery

Melva and I had just enjoyed a wonderful Thanksgiving with her children and grandchildren in Texas. On the day we were leaving to come back home to New Jersey, I noticed that I lost blood when I went to the bathroom.

The next day, everything seemed to be back to normal and I was tempted to just forget about it! However, I decided to get it checked out anyway. A couple of days later the test came back that there was indeed blood in my stools.

That was quite a concern, so we made an appointment to see a gastroenterologist. On Christmas Eve of 2008, he performed an endoscopy and looking down my throat, he found an abscess right where my esophagus met my stomach!

This was an even greater concern. He sent it off to the lab to have it checked to determine whether it was benign or malignant.

On January 4, 2009, we received the report that it was esophageal cancer, and was probably between Stage One and Two. This was a big shock to us newlyweds!

We sat in our kitchen that day and cried together, wondering how we were going to handle this next crisis coming our way.

One of the top oncology surgeons in the state was recommended to us, and several weeks later, I sat in his office while he perused all the test results and finally pronounced, "I would say you have six months to two years to live!"

Melva had an unavoidable ministry engagement that day and could not be there with me for the appointment, so we asked a close friend to go with me. I remember driving home after that appointment, both of us in shock, and literally planning my own funeral!

It was a 'sucker punch!' All that was offered were the standard treatments of chemotherapy, radiation and surgery... and that seemed like a very hard road indeed!

The Sucker Punches of Life

Life is full of sucker punches – unexpected things you don't see coming! You aren't prepared for them; you're caught completely off guard and taken by surprise! And down you go!

However, the failure is not in getting knocked down. As long as you are breathing, that will happen sooner or later. The failure is in staying down and not getting back up again!

It took us a little over a week to pick ourselves up off the floor and begin to come to terms with what lay ahead.

It took us a couple more weeks to disseminate this shattering news to our families, friends, Boards, ministry associates and people in general. And then began the arduous journey to recover and overcome the odds!

Becoming the 'Walking Dead' – 'From the Treatment, Not the Disease!

What followed in the months of February and March that year was the double hit of chemotherapy and radiation simultaneously for six weeks.

The purpose of chemotherapy is to poison your body to the extent that even the cancer thinks it's not a good place to be! Having radiation at the same time is a double whammy!

In my case, I started to become like the 'living dead!' I lost a lot of weight; my appetite was almost completely gone and normal smells seemed foul! Even the smell of water would make me heave!

At one point, I was so sick I thought I wouldn't make it through the night. Melva stayed awake throughout the night, watching to make sure my breathing didn't stop!

Two Rounds of Chemo, Radiation and Major Surgery

The purpose of these treatments was to shrink the tumor in my esophagus so it would be easier to perform the surgery. After the chemo and radiation course was complete, tests showed that had indeed happened. What followed was a little over a month of recuperation until early in May when I was due to have an esophagectomy.

The surgery involved removing eight inches of my esophagus, which in total is only 11 inches long, and pulling up a portion of my stomach to fashion a tube that is then attached to the remaining three inches, effectively replacing the esophagus.

During surgery, the surrounding lymph nodes were checked and one was found to be 'hot,' which meant I would have to follow up with another round of chemo later on.

After 10 days in the hospital in excruciating pain, I went home to recover. After approximately another six weeks, I began the second round of chemo. It was no less brutal, and lasted another five weeks. That took me through to nearly the end of August.

Getting Back On the Road

By mid-September, I was feeling strong enough to get back on the road and continue my traveling ministry, and we started to see a lot of fruit for my efforts. Having been near the 'brink,' I had gained a whole new perspective on life and ministry. I had no compunction whatsoever about using what I had been through to bring glory and honor to God!

As is often common in cancer patients, my six month checkup in January of 2010 revealed that I had two blood clots in my lungs. So I was rushed back into the hospital for three days to have the clots dissolved before they could break off and travel to the brain, possibly causing a stroke!

Throughout 2010, I tried to resume a somewhat normal life. My surgeon had said, in his opinion, I had about a 70-80% chance of surviving five years, and I was hopeful of exceeding those odds.

Cancer Re-occurrence at Stage Four

My weekly schedule always seemed to by taken up with traveling to various churches and conferences and those six month health checkups were all clear, except for the last one in December.

It revealed that there was a rising level of activity in my tumor markers. A short time later, we found out that the cancer had reoccurred in two lymph nodes on the left side of my neck, just above my clavicle.

Once again, my surgeon's report was not good! This was now considered to be Stage Four cancer, with a prognosis of six to 12 months!

So here we were again – another sucker punch!

It took me about another week to pick myself up off the floor again, but it was a little easier the second time.

Two Death Sentences!

That was now two death sentences in two years. Again we had to process the whole thing and inform everyone, friends and family alike, of this latest challenge.

From an orthodox medical point of view, the only solution was more chemotherapy and radiation. I was adamant that chemo was no longer an option for me – been there; done that! It was offered only as a palliative, not a curative solution so, for me, the issue was more one of quality of life over quantity. Additional chemotherapy may have given me a few extra months, but in a 'walking dead' state!

Orthodox or Alternative?

I did, however, seriously consider radiation and was prepared to start a full six week course again, when a friend alerted me to the work of a Christian hospital in Mexico. Founded in the early Sixties, this hospital specialized in integrated treatments.

Western medicine focuses on the tumor, its goal being to destroy the tumor at all cost and will claim a success even if it destroys the patient in the process! This hospital, on the other hand, specialized in treating the whole patient, encouraging the body's own natural defenses to fight off the cancer, boosted by certain natural aids not available in the United States.

If necessary, this would be combined with chemo, surgery and radiation, but only as a last resort. That's why the treatment is termed integrated.

South of the Border

In June of 2011 we made our first trip south of the border for two weeks of treatments. These included intravenous high dosage Vitamin C, vitamin B17 derived from the pits of apricots, a form of artificial blood developed by the Russians, and Ozone treatments.

This last one was interesting. They would draw out a pint of my blood and mix it with ozone through a special machine that looked like a desktop computer, and then put the mixed pint of blood back into my blood stream.

The effect was that the ozone (O_3) would highly oxygenate (O_2) the blood, making it an unfriendly environment for cancer to grow in, because it is anaerobic.

While the blood was going back in, it was run through a UV filter, which would give it greater purity.

All that, accompanied by a mountain of supplements and pills three times a day, along with a semi-vegan diet, was designed to promote greater longevity in cancer patients, and they had the statistics to prove it.

Over the next year, I had four more visits to the Christian Hospital and I'm convinced it helped me outlast the dire prognosis of the doctors stateside!

Part Four – The Shadow of Eternity

In the **Shadow** of **Eternity!**

CHAPTER 17
So, How Should We Live In the Shadow of Eternity?

What Am I Learning?

Just to recap, late in 2008, I was strong and healthy, going to the gym three or four times a week. However, an endoscopy on Christmas Eve that year revealed I had cancer in my esophagus.

In January of 2009, I found myself sitting in an office with a surgeon, who informed me I had only six months to two years to live. How does one deal with that?

I'll not pretend to have all the answers but, in this last section of the book, I would like to share the main things I am in the process of learning.

When your life is interrupted by the unwelcome guest of cancer, many well-intentioned folks ask questions like: "What is God teaching you through all this?" and "You must have learned so much about yourself...?"

You never stop learning, whether sick or well, there is never an end to the educational process of life.

The majority of my friends are much younger than me. I am normally a high energy individual and one of the sources I draw from is youthful enthusiasm!

Intergenerational relationships offer a symbiotic situation where interchanges can bring life-giving benefits to both parties. The young can offer energy to the old, but it is the duty of the old to encourage the young!

Discouragement is everywhere. It does not have to be pursued; it knows your address! However, encouragement has to be ardently sought out and treasured when found.

You will be forgotten for a thousand words of rebuke, but remembered for just one word of encouragement!

Having said all that, several years ago, a young disciple of mine came to me looking for encouragement. He had been discouraged about something and questioned me, "How long will the Lord keep testing me?" I knew what he wanted to hear; however, sometimes it's kinder in the long run to tell people not what they want, but what they need to hear!

"Until your dying breath!" I proclaimed. He was not very encouraged, but that was the truth!

You live and learn... and as long as you are living, you will be learning, even to the last heartbeat!

Here is what I have been learning specific to the life-threatening challenges cancer throws at you, whether you like it or not!

Crucial to Survive

For someone accustomed to traveling in ministry on a weekly basis for over 20 years it was a challenge to be at home for most of that first year.

The standard protocol of western treatment is chemotherapy, radiation and surgery, and that set me on a path for most of 2009 with a hoped for 70% chance of survival over the following five year period.

By the way, I always thought 'therapy' was supposed to be something pleasant, as in 'therapeutic,' but the debilitating effects of chemotherapy grossly and negatively affect every part of your being – physically, spiritually and soulishly. It poisons every part of you!

I found I had to be on my guard against negativity at all times, and I pleaded with the Lord constantly for special grace to bear the treatment. He delivered, and I was grateful!

The strength of His Word, His amazing grace, the prayers of thousands and your own resilience are crucial to survive this kind of trial.

So again, what am I learning? Well, it became obvious that this was a time to get a liberal dose of my own medicine! Since 2009, I have had to literally live out every scripture I have preached to hundreds of congregations all over the world.

Here are a few lessons I have been learning that are essential to anyone going through similar trials:

Day by Day

The first thing I am learning in this situation is you literally have to take one day at a time.

"Therefore do not worry about tomorrow, for tomorrow will worry about its own things. Sufficient for the today is its own trouble" (Matthew 6:34).

When you wake up every morning wondering if you are going to have enough strength to get through the day, your focus becomes just that day! You're not thinking about the next week, next month or next year. Everything is more immediate!

That doesn't mean you are forgetting your dreams, goals or plans, but when you are in a life-threatening crisis, survival demands that your perspective must change so you can make it through, one day at a time!

With no promise of tomorrow, every day's value increases.

Not long ago, I gave an assignment to some students at a Bible School I teach at annually.

Without wishing to be morose, but wanting them to confront a vital, albeit uncomfortable truth in life, I asked them to imagine they had just found out they had only one month to live! Their assignment was to compose a 'bucket list' of all the things they would want to do before their demise.

Naturally, the answers all came back as you might expect – make things right with all those closest to you, make sure to spend time with family and friends, ask for forgiveness of all, do something you've always wanted to do but never had the courage to do before, etc.

And then, reality hit! I told them that nobody knows how long they've got! There's no guarantee of tomorrow for anyone… healthy or sick, rich or poor, young or old.

There's just today! As a matter of fact, every hour is precious, every minute unique; every second that ticks by is one you will never get back; each heartbeat never to be had again! We come with a use-by-date!

It got through to those students that you have to live your life keeping short accounts, working tirelessly for the expansion of the Kingdom of God, but ready to go at any moment and able to give a good account of your life and how, hopefully, it may have glorified God!

A few years ago, I was sharing my testimony of battling cancer during one of my preaching engagements. Afterward, a young guy of sixteen came up to me as I was leaving and declared, "Hey Jeff, you're in your sixties, I'm just 16. I've got a long way to go!"

Now, I knew what he was saying, that he was looking forward to a long stretch ahead. However, a weakness of the young can be an enamoring of their own sense of immortality, not having yet lived long enough to appreciate just how thin the 'silver chord' can be.

So, I just had to say to him, "Last week, within a few days of each other, two young guys around your age, dropped dead from heart failure on basketball courts in Texas! Whether you're 60 or 16, each one of us is only one heart beat away from God's face!"

That floored him and seemed to be a revelation that had never entered his young heart before. He walked away shaking his head, which I hope was letting some light enter.

Walking on Water

The next thing I am learning is to completely trust God not just for *some* things, or to satisfy a current need. I mean in *everything*!

"My friends, I want you to know what a hard time we had in Asia. Our sufferings were so horrible and so unbearable that death seemed certain. In fact, we felt sure that we were going to die. But this made us stop trusting in ourselves and start trusting God, who raises the dead to life. God saved us from the threat of death, and we are sure that He will do it again and again" (2 Corinthians 1:9-10).

When a doctor says you have only six months to two years to live, there can be a fine line between denial and faith.

When I was initially given that prognosis, I had to come to a place of balanced peace, where even though I believed He would not let me perish, I would be just as happy if He decided that it was time to take me home.

That place can be extremely difficult to reach but, with faith and trusting the Word, I got there.

Death and Glory?

I found great help in the last verses of John, chapter 21, where Jesus prophesies to Peter:

"'Most assuredly, I say to you, when you were younger, you girded yourself and walked where you wished; but when you are old, you will stretch out your hands, and another will gird you and carry you where you do not wish.' This He spoke, signifying by what death he would glorify God...'" (emphasis mine).

The perspective of the flesh alone considers death as a failure, but in God's economy, the way we live, and die, has immense value to Him.

Value not in the sense of some sadistic despot waiting for people to pass so He can get something out of it, but how a life lived and died imbued in selflessness has value for eternity.

Our flesh demands survival at all costs! But a God-conscious spirit and soul knows that eternal life remains after this one!

The Flood of Opinion

And then the flood came! Once we let everyone know what was happening, beginning with family, then friends, ministry associates and finally everyone on our lists, multitudes of letters, emails and calls came in!

Most were very supportive, some were rebuking, some were encouraging, and some were very understanding. The plethora of opinions was vast and generally well-intentioned, even if misguided on the odd occasion.

The long list of internet cures grew every day, with exotic remedies from all over the world. Had I opted for that route, I'd still be wading through the list! However, we did try some of the more credible offerings.

Choose Your Weapon

Standing completely on faith was the most prominent strategy presented and I had no argument with that, but I also knew that when you are surrounded by enemies on all sides, you investigate all the options available!

When you go to war, you don't just take your sword; you take a shield, a spear and all kinds of armor to protect you on all sides!

We spent enormous amounts of time evaluating every medical option, from the standard treatments of chemotherapy, radiation and surgery to alternative and integrative treatments, and the course that transpired over the years since this crisis began is the one we felt guided to take.

The course I decided on may not be the right course for everyone. You can't just drop a one-size-fits-all template on everybody, any more than you can ignore the uniqueness of each individual's case. What is important is that those going through a life-threatening situation come to a place of God-given peace in their spirit as to what direction of treatment to pursue.

The Root of All Fear

"We are people of flesh and blood. That is why Jesus became one of us. He died to destroy the devil, who had power over death. But He also died to rescue all of us who live each day in fear of dying" (Hebrews 2:14-15).

The unknown links us to the root of all fear, which cannot be divorced from the future, and in turn begs questions like, "What will happen up ahead?" or "Will it happen again?"

The fear of death is the ultimate expression of the fear of the unknown! To the agnostic, doubt only awaits. The atheist has the most pitiable future – oblivion! Imagine thinking that all you are – relationships, learning, consciousness, loved ones, etc. – all amount to absolutely nothing in the end!

Jesus' ultimate sacrifice took back the keys of Hell and death from the usurper, who had robbed Adam of his legal God-given right to have dominion over creation. Since Christ's victory, the reality is, the enemy became a toothless tiger and for the last 2,000 years has had only one weapon at his disposal – deception!

The great circus magnate, P. T. Barnum is credited as once saying, "There's a sucker born every minute!" And he was right! Our fallen world is based on a lie from the 'father of lies,' and as long as someone is prepared to believe it, the enemy's kingdom maintains a foothold!

In other words, the kingdom of darkness depends almost entirely upon human gullibility, stupidity, and sometimes a stubborn inability to let the light of the simple truth of the gospel shine on through!

Our first father led us to be born into darkness, but the second Adam brought us the light of the gospel to dispel this darkness and set people free!

Free from what?

The real victory Christ offers is not necessarily the elimination of physical death; we know that is a part of life in this world every day.

Of course, we know the end game is to erase the word death from our eternal vocabulary, but the good news of the gospel is that He came to eradicate the ultimate fear of death, which can bind us to this world only, possibly to the point of ignoring the eternal benefits yet to come.

When the realization sinks in that Jesus set us free from the ultimate fear of death, you become fearless. Living or dying pales into insignificance in the shadow of eternity!

I have preached for years that only a true Christian has the win/win hope that whether I live or die, I just can't lose for winning.

"For to me to live is Christ, and to die is gain" (Philippians 1:21).

Since this health crisis began, I have had to literally live out these verses daily in my own life.

Inner Strength

"The spirit of a man will sustain him in sickness..." (Proverbs 18:14).

Your human spirit is partly composed of your genetic makeup, influenced by the choices you make in life, and your environment. This determines whether you have a timid, bold, adventurous, lethargic or energetic spirit. This, in turn, will determine your attitude, which is vitally important to survival.

At the beginning of this trial, during one of my many visits to the hospital for treatment, a nurse said to me, "I've seen a lot of people come and go in your condition, and I can always tell which ones are going to make it and which ones won't... and I know you will!"

A resilient inner strength of spirit is a crucial commodity to survive the negative reports that will come from heaven and earth.

When I say heaven, I don't mean the highest heaven where God's throne dwells, but the lower spiritual realms of dark influence that will whisper lies and deceit, endeavoring to erode your faith, sowing doubt and even condemnation! The battleground is the human mind, and you must stay positive.

A positive attitude is a fertile bed for faith, which along with family and friends, is the most powerful antidote to any life-threatening disease or any other crisis situation.

Life Jacket

"I have learned, in whatsoever state I am, therewith to be content" (Philippians 4:11).

The challenging changes I've experienced since 2009 have had some disastrous results for others, both financially as well as physically.

In all of this, the above scripture has been a life jacket in an uncertain sea.

The support the Lord has provided through His Body has been enough to relieve us of the stress associated with the loss of regular income from ministry and preaching. Even the uninsured costs of integrated treatments outside the country, totaling thousands of dollars, have been completely covered!

However, the Lord's provision has only been available directly in line with His law of sowing and reaping. Directing my ministry efforts and life primarily into the Northeast of America for the 10 years leading up to the beginning of this health crisis, pouring into leaders, churches and people, and building strong relationships produced a harvest of provision in a time of great need.

Dealing with the stress of the disease is enough without having to be concerned about support, and my gratitude to the Lord cannot be adequately expressed!

Apart from all that, there's a time and season for everything. I am forever thankful for God's amazing grace that got me this far!

These have been some hard lessons, and that's just some of what I am learning!

In the **Shadow** of **Eternity!**

CHAPTER 18
Looking Ahead

Holding the Line of Honor to God, No Matter What!

Arthur Stace, otherwise known as Mr. Eternity, was an Australian reformed alcoholic who converted to Christianity and spread the gospel by writing the word "Eternity" in chalk on footpaths in Sydney over a period of approximately 35 years from the 1930s until the 1960s.

In the early Thirties, Stace heard a sermon that would ultimately change the course of his life. It was based on Isaiah 57:15, "For thus says the High and Lofty One, Who inhabits eternity, Whose name is Holy: 'I dwell in the high and holy place, with him who has a contrite and humble spirit, to revive the spirit of the humble....'"

Arthur Stace

A One Word Sermon

In a much later interview, Stace would say, "Eternity went ringing through my brain and suddenly I began crying and felt a powerful call from the Lord to write Eternity." Even though he was illiterate and could hardly write his own name legibly, "the word 'Eternity' came out smoothly, in a beautiful copperplate script. I couldn't understand it, and I still can't," he said.

It is estimated that he wrote the word somewhere around 500,000 times over those 35 years.

Today, Stace's one word sermon has become an Australian national icon and is memorialized on a plaque at Sydney Town Hall. As a tribute to Stace, the Sydney Harbour Bridge was lit up with the word "Eternity" as part of the 1999 New Year's Eve celebrations marking the beginning of the new Millennium.

A Shadow of the Real

A shadow is merely an outline of a real object. There is shape, but no detail. Life is but a shadow of eternity. What we think is real now will pale into insignificance with all that waits beyond. We all meet eternity eventually – be ready, but not in a rush!

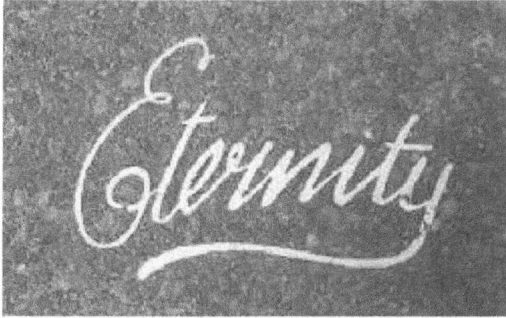

The Eternity plaque at Sydney Town Hall

The End Is the Beginning

I love life, and I'm in no hurry to get to the next level. Eternity has no measure; time does not exist. Eternity is God's habitation. According to the scriptures, Hell is a place of torment, but the greatest torture would be to be forever separated from God's presence!

We have forever to spend in eternity, but what matters most is the mark we leave here in this world that will lead others to spend forever with their Creator. Our lives can only be truly measured by the fruit we take with us from this world. That fruit is souls!

Producing fruit does not just involve winning people to the Lord and then that's the end of it! We also have to inspire, encourage, and strengthen others along the journey to make sure they stay the course to the end – which is actually just the beginning!

In this digital age, where we continually live with information overload, it's amazing how one illiterate man from last century with a one word graffiti message can still be impacting us today. That's because Arthur Stace's "Eternity" is timeless!

Living In the Shadow of Eternity

My life currently is a daily struggle to preserve my health so that I can accomplish all the Lord would have me do, living in the shadow of eternity.

Perhaps this book is my final assignment. But I've been wrong before, thinking I had completed my mission with previous tasks. However, to complete this work leaves me with a strong sense of accomplishment... that I have finished the life's work He set before me.

If I am ever again asked the question of having any unfinished assignments to complete, I now have the confidence to answer "no!"

There has been a multitude of correspondence from people all over the world saying that I have become an example to them of how to endure... through trials of health, crisis and more.

Here is just one example of the many:

"You have been great about staying positive in your walk, it is not an easy walk. But I need you to know that the attitude you have is what and how others are making it through their situations!

If they can borrow you as their example even as you walk through this, it gives hope and adds the faith that many people just don't have.

Faith of a mustard seed is all that is needed. As God will and can use any circumstance, I pray that is what this season is for you. I will believe that a new season is coming of restoration for you physically. Spiritually the changes you are making will be a great benefit to you and for the future of your ministry.

I believe with you and in agreement for all God's best in you and your family's lives, personal family and church family!"

I am very mindful of that and feel a great responsibility to the Lord to set and maintain this example in a way that honors Him.

What is left for me is to hold fast to the call of God, even in these dire circumstances, living in the face of suffering and holding the line of honor to God, no matter what happens... complete miracle of healing or not! It's all been a miracle for me anyway! Everything!

I have told several people close to me that whatever you do, don't make a hero out of me. The more that would happen, the less honor God receives, and honoring Him is the priority!

My life, flawed as it has been, can only begin to make sense in light of any redemptive activity accomplished in the hearts of those whose paths divinely crossed with mine. If there is any value, then that is it! It's the difference between "wood, hay and stubble" and rich, pure, eternal gold.

So the legacy I hope to leave and see endure should be found in the hearts of changed lives for Christ, where people have caught a glimpse of Jesus and hung onto it, producing fruit... hopefully to a great degree.

As I progress in this season, that's what is left for me to do. And it is enough!

In the **Shadow** of **Eternity!**

Postscript

On August 8, 2013 at 5:41 pm, Jeff Beacham left the confines of earth and moved home to Heaven. His sons, Samuel and Jacob, and I (Melva) were with him, speaking blessings and release to him as he passed.

It was his heart's desire to finish strong, to finish well; and indeed, he did. Jeff finished just as he had lived; not shrinking back from adversity, but pressing through against the odds; in everything, praying that his life would be an inspiration to others and bring honor to God.

Following a year of reprieve, the cancer returned and metastasized in his lymph nodes, lungs, spine and pelvis. It was a peculiar time. We both strongly believed that God still performs miracles today, and had personally experienced, and prayed for others to receive, them. But as we prayed about this latest diagnosis, neither of us had an unction of the Holy Spirit to press for more time. On the contrary, Jeff had an urgency to complete anything left unfinished and run for the finish line!

Instead of becoming bitter, he became increasingly thankful, profoundly grateful for each day of life – the glorious wonder of sunsets through our kitchen window; the profuse, pink blossoms blanketing our cherry tree; the sweet innocence and delightful laughter of our grandchildren; and the companionship of faithful, loyal friends.

Over the years as Jeff ministered to pastors, his recurring question to them had been, "Who is your Timothy?" How often his heart was grieved to hear them reply, "I have no one."

Jeff believed that often the vision God gives an individual to fulfill is too big for one generation to accomplish. It must be prayerfully handed off to the next generation. But without the right successor, a leader's vision and life's work will perish at his demise. That's why Jeff so passionately urged those within his circle of influence to search out their "Timothy" early on, and mentor them to a successful future.

No wonder then, one of Jeff's foremost finishing goals was to designate a successor to lead Firepower Ministries, International. One of his spiritual sons, Joshua Kennedy, shared his passion for reawakening in the Northeast and his burden for the next generation. In his last months of life, Jeff carefully poured into Joshua his vision of the Great Wheel of Reawakening, and subsequently entrusted FMI to his care.

"I am honored that Jeff saw fit to pass his mantle on to me," said Joshua. "During his celebration service and hours after, my wife, Loraine, and I felt God's amazing presence and Holy Spirit working in our hearts. What was on Jeff was transferred to me in a tangible way.

A mighty warrior has left this earth, yet the legacy of this great man will live on through those whom he inspired.

Now my generation will carry the vision of the Great Wheel of Reawakening forward.

Jeff and I shared this similar passion and I am totally committed to 'advancing the front line.' To me, Jeff is like Moses. He pressed the Kingdom forward in his generation, yet did not see the completion of his vision. But my name is Joshua, and I and my generation have been created to slay giants and conquer the land. We will press the Kingdom forward until we see this prophetic vision fulfilled."

Jeff, you fought the good fight, you finished your race, you kept the faith. Now there is laid up for you the crown of righteousness, which the Lord, the righteous Judge, will give to you on Judgment Day! (2 Tim. 4:7-8)

Joshua, you are surrounded by a great cloud of witnesses, Jeff being among them. Run, then, with endurance, the race that is set before you, looking unto Jesus, the Author and Finisher of your faith. (Heb. 12:1-2) You will overcome! (Rev. 12:11)

As Jeff so often said, "We are all just one heartbeat from seeing the face of God." God grant us grace to live each day with the word ETERNITY emblazoned across our minds!

For the honor of HIS great name,
Melva Beacham
www.melvaleaministries.org
melva@melvalea.org
214.432.0505

To bring this Great Wheel of Reawakening to your region or
partner with this vision, contact:
Joshua Kennedy
President/CEO
Firepower Ministries International
609.402.8869
www.firepowerministries@live.com

In the **Shadow** of **Eternity!**

In the **Shadow** of **Eternity!**

We have published over 1,800 books. We still consider new books. We prayerfully choose our books. Send Manuscript to bill.vincent@yahoo.com.

We will respond in 10 days or less.

We distribute books to all of the key retailers in the country including Amazon, Barnes & Noble, Borders, Books-A-Million, Baker & Taylor, Ingram and all of the Christian trade (Family, LifeWay, Mardel, Christian Book Distributors, Send the Light, etc.)

Fast, Quality, Expanding Publishing Services

Revival Waves of Glory Books & Publishing
Books for God's Glory
http://www.stl-distribution.com/vendors/?id=7639

Revival Waves of Glory Ministries
Bill Vincent Author/President
PO Box 596
Litchfield, IL 62056
www.revivalwavesofgloryministries.com

In the **Shadow** of **Eternity!**

www.ingramcontent.com/pod-product-compliance
Lightning Source LLC
Chambersburg PA
CBHW021827090426
42811CB00032B/2063/J